Working Hard & Working WELL

Advance Praise for Working Hard & Working Well

"David Hunter's blueprint for linking accountability with sustainability is a must-read for leaders, mid-level managers, and front-line staff. Hunter's philosophy on the 'theory of change' can help social-sector organizations bridge the gap between idealism and strategy to operations and logistics."

—Pat Lawler, CEO, Youth Villages

"David helped Roca develop and refine our theory of change and use it as an operational blueprint to implement our performance-management system and to support our strategic growth plans. Most important, he helped us get better at what we do so that we can be worthy of the young people we have the privilege of serving. *Working Hard—and Working Well* captures the passion and integrity of David's approach. It is a practical 'how to' guide for organizations committed to high performance and will become an indispensable must-read resource in the social sector."

—Molly Baldwin, Executive Director, Roca, Inc.

"I regard David Hunter as one of the most serious and thoughtful people working to improve the social sector. His unique theory-of-change workshops have helped many organizations transform themselves into high-performing agencies that deliver outcomes to service recipients as intended—measurably, reliably, and sustainably. *Working Hard—and Working Well* is a sage book, written simply, straightforwardly, and with David's well-known passion."

—Michael Bailin, former President, Edna McConnell Clark Foundation

"David Hunter draws upon his extraordinary experience to present a thoughtful, compelling case for the importance of performance management as well as a practical guide for how to implement effective processes in real-life settings. Accordingly, this book will be an invaluable resource for anyone determined to deliver strong results in a nonprofit or public agency."

—Paul Carttar, former Director, Social Innovation Fund

"In clear and powerful language, Hunter draws on his decades of experience as a nonprofit CEO, foundation evaluator, and consultant to give those who lead and work with human services organizations a tangible way forward. To read this book is to hope that all human services organizations, and those that fund them, would embrace its recommendations—and to wonder how many millions of people's lives would be improved, even saved, if they did."

—Phil Buchanan, President, Center for Effective Philanthropy

Working Hard & Working WELL

A Practical Guide to

PERFORMANCE MANAGEMENT

FOR LEADERS SERVING
CHILDREN, ADULTS, AND FAMILIES

David E. K. Hunter

A SLEEVES-ROLLED-UP COMPANION TO *LEAP OF REASON*

ISBN: 978-0-9886180-1-5 (PDF edition), 978-0-9886180-0-8 (Kindle edition), 978-0-9886180-2-2 (iBook edition)

To my wife, Elaine, and our daughter, Lisa, whom I cherish and who together have made me a better person

And to those who work with passion and dedication to help others lead better lives with better prospects

Contents

Preface

by Steve Butz, CEO and Founder, Social Solutions, Inc.

David Hunter and I met about fifteen years ago, shortly after my company launched the Efforts to Outcomes (ETO)® performance-management data system. At the time David was the Director of Assessment and Knowledge Development at the Edna McConnell Clark Foundation, and he was looking for a system he could recommend to the foundation's grantees. David expressed an appreciation for what ETO could do. But it will not surprise anyone who knows David that he also found many things about it to critique—much the way he does when engaged with organizations as a consultant who is relentlessly focused on helping them build the capacity to "manage to outcomes." Like them, we have listened to what David had to say (even when it hurt) and have benefitted greatly from David's advice, both formal and informal. ETO is much the better for it.

Over the years since then, David has developed and refined his unique Theory of Change Workshops to help social service organizations build their performance management capacity. Many of America's most outstanding social service agencies—and some foundations too—have benefitted from their engagements with him. He's the ultimate gadfly in our sector, challenging all of us to keep in mind that, ultimately, the only way we can justify our existence is by meaningfully and measurably advancing the wellbeing and life prospects of the people who turn to nonprofit and public services for inspiration, help, and support.

As David began to move into a retirement mode, he wanted to leave behind a book that would continue to help the social sector develop, become more effective, and even become more efficient. He wanted the book to be accessible to anybody and everybody who had an interest in contributing to these developments, although he wasn't sure how to go about doing so.

And then Mario Morino stepped forward. Hearing what David was trying to do, he encouraged David to write a book—not just any kind of book, but one that was very concrete, filled with specific examples of his work and practical advice grounded in his experiences. In short, he suggested that David offer a meaty "how to" manual rather than a bugle blast or call to action. Then, putting deeds behind his words, Mario generously put an incredible team to work to support David. Lowell Weiss led the process; Cheryl Collins served as general editor; Katya Rice as copyeditor; and Chris Wright took the manuscript and converted it into a publishable format. Their collective efforts resulted in David's e-book Working Hard—and Working Well: A Practical Guide to Performance Management, a natural complement to Mario's highly influential Leap of Reason: Managing to Outcomes in an Era of Scarcity.

Recently, the opportunity presented itself to join with Mario in helping David share his message. I am delighted that Social Solutions has taken the step to support the publication of this hardcover edition of Working Hard—and Working Well. We do so not only to celebrate David's work and notable contributions to the sector, but also out of a sense of pride—because most of the organizations that he discusses in this book also happen to use ETO to support their efforts to deliver effective services to their clients, services that deliver the outcomes they promise. We continue to work hard to make ETO ever more flexible and easy to use so that implementing a performance-management system will not be an obstacle to organizations seeking to develop the capacity to manage to outcomes, but an exciting and valued component of doing so.

We are proud to be members of the Leap of Reason community doing our share to build a strong, reliable, sustainable, and effective social sector.

Baltimore, MD
August, 2013

Foreword

by Mario Morino, Chairman, Venture Philanthropy Partners

In *Working Hard—and Working Well*, David Hunter generously shares the successful processes he has developed over three decades to help nonprofit leaders find their North Star. His rigorous approach leads them to gain clarity about what they do and to confirm that what they do makes a measurable, meaningful, and lasting difference for the children and families they serve.

I met David in late 2000 through Mike Bailin, the laser-focused and very smart president of the Edna McConnell Clark Foundation (EMCF). At the time, EMCF was well along in its transformation from traditional foundation to a highly strategic and performance-based change-maker. David, as EMCF's director of assessment and knowledge development, was one of Mike's secret weapons.

As my colleagues and I at Venture Philanthropy Partners began to interact more with the team at EMCF, we got to know David better. We had heard some of the legendary stories of David's wrath and his refusal to drink the field's Kool-Aid. It turned out the stories were true. You see, David tells it like it is, very bluntly, without apology. From the beginning I loved his directness.

My appreciation for David grew shortly after EMCF co-invested with Venture Philanthropy Partners in the Maya Angelou Public Charter School. As part of the investment process, David conducted a three-day theory-of-change workshop for the Maya Angelou team.

David's performance earned raves from my colleagues, including some who went in as true nonbelievers. My colleagues also acknowledged that having David lead a theory-of-change session is, in and of itself, a sign of leadership courage—given how tough he can be.

David comes by his tough-love approach honestly. As you will see in David's account in Chapter 2 ("Why I Take Performance Management Personally"), twenty-one years ago he was thrown into the deep end when he was put in charge of a dysfunctional state psychiatric hospital. On the first day of his tenure, he saw that the hospital was falling far short of living up to its mission of providing high-quality care to patients, many of whom were at risk of causing harm to themselves, other patients, or their healthcare providers.

The hospital's lack of performance was not an abstract or purely academic concern. It was a life-and-death challenge. Instead of sprinting for the hills, David ran into the breach. He turned the hospital around, despite every imaginable organizational challenge.

Two years ago, it was my turn to be the courageous leader. I invited David to be an essayist for *Leap of Reason*. I did so with some trepidation, not knowing if I was ready for his uncompromising ways. Thank God I did. David not only contributed a powerful essay; he also offered countless suggestions for improving my essay—and, yes, admonished me when I veered off or went too soft. David helped make the book much better, and I am grateful.

But it wasn't until after we released *Leap of Reason*, when my team and I visited some of the best nonprofits in their fields, that I fully grasped David's brilliance. On each visit, as I dug deeper into the culture and performance of these nonprofits, a common thread emerged—David Hunter was providing sage strategic counsel to all of them.

David helps turn on light bulbs for the leaders fortunate enough to work with him. Yes, his approach generates some heat. But by the end of one of his sessions, the process almost always produces far more light than heat. The leaders I met couldn't have given David more praise for how he helped them. They literally love him. And I understand why.

David is now getting ready to hang up his spurs and head into retirement. And that's why I am so enthusiastic and thankful that he has documented his approach for all the members of our sector who are brave enough to ensure that they do what they say they do. In *Working Hard—and Working Well*, David gives the recipe for the "secret sauce" behind his famous workshops. He offers a template that other skilled facilitators and leaders can use to augment their own work with organizations motivated to make the leap of reason. Ultimately, I hope it provides some of the DNA necessary for cloning his effective approach and producing a host of rigorous, tough-minded David Hunters in our field.

Rocky River, OH
December 2012

Author's Note

This book represents what I have learned over the course of some three decades of leading, managing, and consulting to organizations and programs in both the public and nonprofit sectors, where I worked to build organizational competencies and capacity to improve the lives and prospects of marginalized, weakened, or otherwise disempowered individuals, families, groups, communities, and populations. Since I am addressing a wide audience with differing levels of exposure to the discipline of performance management, I will err on the side of explaining at a level of detail that will help newcomers to this approach understand and implement it. Nevertheless, I hope that this document will also be of interest and use to those with greater experience in this area, and that especially the examples of the work of front-line organizations will be a valuable resource and inspiration to them.

Early experiences that led to my approach to performance management came from working in or leading social service institutions and agencies. I refined my thinking and practices in the last decade and a half while consulting to an extraordinary group of public and nonprofit organizations (both direct-service agencies and funders). And it is to these organizations—their leaders, managers, and front-line staff—that I offer my heartfelt thanks for the opportunities they gave me to work with them, learn from them, and enjoy the trust they invested in me. But ultimately this document is dedicated to the people who depend on the quality and effectiveness of the services and supports provided by such organizations—the agencies on which they rely to help them change their lives for the better.

I hope that this will be a useful guide for those who are interested in understanding performance management, those who want to learn how to develop performance-management systems, and those who are looking for practical knowledge about how to implement such systems in order to "manage to outcomes," as Mario Morino puts it so well in his book *Leap of Reason.* I think of it as a "how-to" manual for leaders, managers, and staff working in direct-service organizations to help them work reliably and sustainably at high levels of quality, efficiency, and effectiveness. I hope it will also be useful to organizational consultants occupied in the area of performance management. The text is resolutely practical, a synthesis of my experiences into a matter-of-fact approach to both strategic and tactical (day-to-day) performance management.

I write this book as I move toward retirement, hoping to leave behind a resource for those who work in, fund, and consult to direct-service organizations. It is a book I write with some sadness, because it is a response to my perception that the social sector has failed, so far, to live up to its promise. While hundreds of thousands of social service organizations work incredibly hard to help structurally disadvantaged and socially marginalized individuals, families, and groups build better lives and life prospects for themselves and their children, few do so effectively—and indeed lack the organizational competencies and capacity to do so. This is a bitter truth. And though it is a collective failure—not only of these organizations, but also of their funders and consultants—it is also a correctable one. That is why, in the end, this is a forward-looking, even optimistic undertaking. I have held nothing back. I give numerous examples, and at times I share observations that reflect what I have learned with my sleeves rolled up—while working in and leading social service organizations, and also during my subsequent career as a consultant to them and to funders.

I began writing this book in 2011, more as a way to think through and refine my approach than with any thought of publishing the results. Gradually I discussed what I was doing with various colleagues and was encouraged to turn it into a manual that others could use. That escalated the expectations with which I approached this, and thus the time it required. I am very grateful to Public/Private Ventures for having supported my final drive to pull this into shape so that I could begin to share it and solicit feedback. (When P/PV, an institution that contributed so much to the social sector, had to close its doors, we all suffered a great loss.) Because of my great respect for **Mario Morino**, who has emerged as one of the most articulate and persuasive advocates for the need to support nonprofit organizations in building their capacity to "manage to outcomes," as well as my earlier involvement with his indispensable book *Leap of Reason*, I asked him and his colleague **Lowell Weiss** to read the manuscript. Both were very gracious in encouraging me to bring this effort into publishable form, and Mario was amazingly generous in offering to take on the costs of doing so. Together they assembled a superb team of professionals. Lowell, assisted by **Cheryl Collins**, served as general editor and was especially helpful in pushing for clarity of thought and streamlining the logical flow of chapters and elements. **Katya Rice** took on the painstaking work of copyeditor, **Chris Wright** the details of book design. And finally, I want to acknowledge my dear friend **Michael Bailin**, a pioneer and seminal thinker in transforming philanthropy into effective social investing during his tenure as president of the Edna McConnell Clark Foundation. He recruited me into philanthropy and consultation and gave me a platform from which I could undertake the various streams of work that ultimately led to the creation of this volume.

Many people who work in the social sector have suggested that it would be good to have some easy-to-apply tools that organizations could use to assess their strengths and their capacity for managing performance, and also to chart the areas that need further development. Similarly, there is great interest in knowing when an organization is ready to undertake an evaluation, either formative or summative. I recently developed such tools and tested them; described in Appendix III, they are web-based and available on my website: www.dekhconsulting.com.

A final note: I intend this document to be an admonishment to those funders who demand performance in which they don't invest, results for which they don't pay, and accountability from which they exempt themselves. Stop the madness!

CHAPTER 1

Too Important to Fail

For many nonprofit leaders, "performance management" conjures up the most dehumanizing practices of the corporate sector and reeks of rampant data gathering run amok. This unfortunate association is understandable, given how the concept has emerged and been applied over the last couple of decades. While performance management is often a subject for discussion by leading organizational researchers and consultants, the literature on it has not been particularly accessible or compelling to social service practitioners—or to their funders. The big exceptions, of course, are Jim Collins and his *Good to Great* (2001), followed by his classic text about nonprofit management, *Good to Great and the Social Sectors* (2005). And recently Mario Morino caught the attention of the nonprofit and philanthropic sectors with his *Leap of Reason: Managing to Outcomes in an Era of Scarcity* (2011).

One of the reasons why performance management has failed to excite the social sector is that since its introduction early in the twentieth century it has been used mostly in a top-down, command-and-control approach in order to ensure that whatever work the authorities decreed should get done actually *would* get done. Thus, performance management was a way to drive activities, not results. This phase in the history of performance management can be thought of as "compliance management"—and the phase is not merely a thing of the past, as it continues to thrive in the often excessive metrics used by funders to hold the organizations they support accountable.

Eventually, however, people began to ask themselves to what purpose an organization's activities were being delivered, and thus began to focus on results. This was a major step forward in theory. In practice, though, the idea that social service providers should be able to demonstrate outcomes for program participants has often been used by funders to bludgeon agencies rather than help them improve. Very few funders appreciate what outcomes monitoring and management entails, much less how to help the organizations they support develop the competencies and capacities to adopt such practices.

Performance Management: What It Is and What It Takes

Given the confusion and angst around—and misuse of—the term "performance management," it behooves us to begin with some clear definitions.

An **organization** is a complex, adaptive system—a recognizable combination of elements (such as people and their interrelationships, the resources they use, and the conditions they create for working together) that are interconnected and hence continuously affect one another. And, however explicitly or implicitly, these elements are organized to achieve a set of goals or purposes.

Like all human systems, an organization is not cut off from its environment. Rather, it both affects and is affected by the context within which it works. Consequently, to survive, the organization must monitor what it is doing and what results (intended and unintended) it is producing—and make adaptive changes as its leaders and staff learn from experience.

Organizational performance is the extent to which an entity is able to achieve the goals it has set itself through intentional actions within the contexts in which it works. Performance can be good or bad, effective or ineffective, successful or unsuccessful, well managed or not. Periodic stock-taking enables the organization to learn from what it has and hasn't accomplished, develop an understanding of the reasons for these results, and make adjustments in its operating assumptions, structure, internal systems and processes, personnel, resource utilization, and so on—and thereby to improve its ability to meet the targets it has set itself. Such stock-taking and adjusting is the core of performance management.

Based on how frequently one collects and monitors data and how swiftly one introduces adjustments to improve results, performance management can be either tactical or strategic in nature. Any high-performing organization needs to be good at both and to keep them fully aligned.

Tactical performance management consists of monitoring activities and their results on a day-to-day basis, with small feedback loops to help those on the front lines make adjustments to their work in "real time" in order to achieve the results for which they are held accountable. Inherently, then, tactical performance management requires frequent measurements to monitor day-to-day activities and the incremental ways they affect organizational performance. It focuses on each event of consequence. And it focuses on the people who participate in each event, specifically (a) those who provide services, supports, and opportunities, and (b) the intended beneficiaries (clients). Tactical performance management, therefore, requires a "unit of analysis" that is specific and particular and geared to monitoring how each client is being served and how he or she is (or isn't) benefiting on a day-to-day basis.

While informed by large organizational priorities (strategic performance goals), tactical performance management is a disaster if managed in a top-down, command-and-control manner. The best tactical performance management is *guided self-management at the front lines.* What does this mean? It means that managers give front-line workers accountability for results and the freedom to use their creativity to achieve them.

Tactical Performance Management: Prolonging Life in the Management of Cystic Fibrosis

A good example of tactical performance management comes from Dr. Atul Gawande, the brilliant surgeon and respected author who published a discussion of cystic fibrosis (CF) in the *New Yorker* in 2004. Cystic fibrosis is genetically inherited and, left untreated, results in death by around age seven. Children's lungs become so filled with mucus that they can no longer absorb enough oxygen to sustain life.

Fortunately, we know how to treat CF to extend life dramatically using a few simple means:

1. Monitor one basic metric: the individual's functional lung capacity (the volume of air that can be inhaled into lung space where oxygen can be absorbed into the blood)
2. Make four interventions:
    - Prescribe pancreatic enzyme pills to reduce mucus production in the lungs.
    - Prescribe inhalant medicines that stimulate coughing to expel mucus from the lungs.
    - Maximize caloric intake to help the body fight infection.
    - Provide for daily percussive therapy: using either a motorized vest to shake the chest or cupped hands to strike the torso at each of fourteen locations, stimulate deep coughing that will expel mucus from the lungs.

At 117 CF centers across the United States, this metric is used to monitor each patient's lung capacity and decide how intensively (at what dosage levels) the four elements of the intervention should be utilized as lung capacity either holds constant or drops—and if it drops too far or too fast, at what point hospitalization is indicated. This strategy results in patients' achieving an average life expectancy of about thirty-three years. In other words, this strategy for managing CF adds about twenty-six years to a person's life. It would take a "glass is half empty" type of thinker to dismiss such a dramatic outcome.

Yet, at seven CF centers that use the same strategy for managing the disease, the results are dramatically different: participating patients achieve an average life expectancy of about *fifty* years! All of a sudden thirty-three doesn't look so good. Consider where *you* would want someone you love to receive treatment.

How can we explain the difference?

While at most centers CF is conceived of as a **genetically inherited disease** (which indeed it is), at the seven centers with the longer life expectancy it is viewed as a **degenerative disease** (which it also is), and in these centers the urgent task, day in and day out, is preventing degeneration—that is, preventing loss of lung capacity. Thus, while the focus in the majority of centers is on **patient compliance with treatment**, the focus at the high-performing centers is on the **accountability of staff within the patient-staff dyad to help prevent loss of lung capacity and to drive patient compliance**; and while the former centers **respond reactively** to evidence of lost lung capacity, the latter aim for **proactive prevention**.

That's it. All the techniques and treatment methods are the same. The only difference is tactical performance management with results-driven objectives.

Strategic performance management consists of monitoring activities and their results in aggregated ways over extended periods of time (usually quarterly or yearly). It uses large feedback loops to drive learning and identify needed adjustments that, while infrequent, are more substantial in nature than those required by tactical performance management. Typical examples of strategic performance management for a direct-service provider include such things as maintaining program quality and effectiveness while replicating it at new sites. For a funder it includes selecting investment domains and deciding on and implementing the criteria for choosing grantees.

IN FOCUS

Strategic Performance Management: Our Piece of the Pie® Makes a Key Strategic Decision

As late as 2004, Our Piece of the Pie (OPP), headquartered in Hartford, CT, was still known as Southend Community Services. The organization described itself at that time as a multi-service agency whose mission was to "promote independence and economic success through innovative programs and services in the Greater Hartford, CT, area." Although it saw its youth services as the core of its approach—including case management and social enterprises where young people worked at such things as boat and furniture building and graphic arts, received wages, and were trained in work-readiness skills—the agency also offered programs that did not serve this population. One was its Elderly Services, which operated a Senior Center and provided services to homebound elderly Hartford residents. Another was its Childcare Services, which consisted of three licensed and accredited childcare programs that admitted children without any consideration of the organization's strategic priorities.

Then, at a watershed moment in the theory-of-change workshop that I was facilitating with key staff members, board representatives, agency leaders, and consultants, the agency adopted a revised mission: **"Helping urban youth become successful adults."**

But did the organization's new mission fit with its diffuse programming? After I posed this question, Bob Rath, the president/CEO, stood up and said, "OK, folks. We have been serving these very important and underserved populations because there is a great need and because we know how to do it well. But that doesn't mean we should continue to serve them."

There was a stunned silence in the room, not least because the managers and staff of these two programs were present.

"I've been waiting ten years to push for a more intense focus on youth," Bob continued, "and now is the moment. We are a youth service agency. We are running our Elderly Services because it is a legacy program—in fact, it was our first program—and we're good at it. And we are running Childcare Services because we get paid to do so. But they have nothing to do with our mission now. They are peripheral at best."

The question now became: What should be done about this?

After a frank (and painful) discussion in which workshop participants went so far as to consider cutting these programs, the group decided in the end to bring them into alignment with the agency's newly formulated youth development mission. Thus it decided to limit access to Childcare Services to the children of teenage mothers already in its case-management program. Having reliable access to childcare would provide critical support to these mothers, who would then have fewer constraints on going to school and participating in the agency's programming.

Similarly, while keeping its "youth chore elderly services component," the group decided to redesign it as one more social enterprise work-readiness training venue, alongside the others that the agency already operated. The youth workers would be recruited from among the participants in the agency's case-management program. They would be closely supervised, not only to assess the quality of their services but also to ensure that they were building skills toward work readiness.

But these decisions were provisional. As Bob noted, they would have to be tested: the agency would have to monitor the redesigned programs in action and see how well they were in fact contributing to the agency's youth-development focus. Thus these were not simply decisions of expedience.

In my experience, it is rare for an organization to reach such strategic clarity. It is even rarer for it to have the courage to challenge the continued relevance of its legacy programs and services. This case is a testament to Bob Rath's leadership and to the core of dedicated managers and staff who stuck with the agency as it became more and more focused on driving positive youth outcomes.

After several years, rigorous monitoring of operations made it clear that neither the childcare program nor the youth-chore component of Elderly Services was being utilized well, and neither was needed to drive OPP's youth-development outcomes. **Ultimately, OPP transferred six hundred clients, thirty employees, and nearly $1 million to three local nonprofits that had a better fit between these services and their missions.**

OPP has done an admirable job with its focus on youth development. **Since 2005, 85 percent of OPP's revenues are new and entirely dedicated to its mission.** The agency has continued to refine its Pathways to Success model, has sharpened its educational and employment services, and has partnered with the Hartford public school system in designing and implementing Opportunity High School (a school for over-age, under-credited youths). OPP tracks short-term, intermediate, and long-term outcomes for all the young people it serves, and has won foundation support for a rigorous formative evaluation that, if all goes well, will become the foundation for a summative evaluation of its impacts.

Tactical performance management must be conducted within the guidelines set by strategic performance expectations—and strategic performance expectations must be appropriately framed so that they can be executed on the ground with available resources and within the existing scope of control. But no matter how well conceived an organization's approach to strategic performance management, the proverbial rubber meets the road at the level of tactical performance management. Here is where services work or not, where service recipients actually benefit or not. In a nutshell: Strategic performance management creates the performance context and expectations. Tactical performance management delivers the goods.[1]

Performance Management in the Social Sector: A Brief History

As I noted earlier, neither kind of performance management—tactical or strategic—is a new concept. Although still not widely understood or practiced within the social sector, both kinds have been part of the interplay between government and this sector for more than two decades. A brief tour through history will help clarify the antecedents to performance management and how it has emerged in its present shape.

In America, especially after the Revolution of 1776, functions that had once been mostly under the auspices of the church gradually moved to civic organizations and local government. Almshouses were built to house the poor and disabled; formerly private or church-based institutions of higher learning were put under the authority of government; and better-off families were paid stipends to help the less fortunate. At the same time, government began to rely on organized charities to perform essential tasks that were beyond its own

1. As we will see shortly, strategic performance management is a leadership function; tactical performance management, a management function. Both are essential. When dealing with services to human beings, how one drives organizational and staff performance both strategically and tactically can make the difference between life and death.

capacities—as in the case of the U.S. Sanitary Commission, which, among other things, provided health services on battlefields.

In a watershed moment after World War II, America turned with ideological finality away from becoming a European-style welfare state. While the government experienced steady growth on a rich diet of universal taxation, public policies encouraged the emergence of nonprofit organizations to provide direct services (paid for by public funds) to targeted populations that were deemed in need of, and worthy of, such services. Until well beyond the middle of the twentieth century, public performance management focused entirely on the measurement of public needs as a context for allocating resources, and on the monitoring of activities paid for by the government to address these needs.

Eventually, however, policymakers began to ask "So what?"—the idea being that hard work was not in itself a public good. Rather, they realized, hard work was the means through which public good could be produced. In other words, the issue became not what was *done* with public funds but what was *accomplished*. Or, to use the language of today, the focus shifted to results, to outcomes.

In 1993 Congress passed, and the President signed into law, the U.S. Government Program Results Act (GPRA). This exquisitely brief (twelve-page) and trenchant piece of legislation was designed "to provide for the establishment of strategic planning and performance measurement in the Federal Government" in the context of limited resources and the conviction that expenditures must therefore be tied to results. Specifically, GPRA was intended to:

- Solve the problem of lack of adequate information about government performance
- Address waste and inefficiency
- Provide a framework for understanding the effectiveness of government programs
- Build public trust in the government
- Introduce accountability for results into the public sector

Under GPRA, federal agencies had five years to implement the requirements of the law and thus to develop the means to demonstrate the results of their programs and services. They were encouraged to use pilot projects to test performance-measurement strategies, but few did so, and most were caught unprepared when the legal requirements became active in 1998. This led to hasty implementation efforts that were mostly top-down, poorly thought through, and not created with the involvement of key (including local) constituencies.

Since its introduction, GPRA has had some good consequences and also some unfortunate ones. Here are a few of each.

GPRA: Good consequences

- Very significant amounts of public resources are committed to evaluating government programs and services (through the U.S. Office of Policy and Management, the U.S. Government Accountability Office, and research commissioned and supported through the various federal departments and agencies such as the U.S. Department of Labor and the U.S. Department of Education's Institute of Education Sciences).
- Results of government evaluations are made accessible to the public and inform public policy debates.
- A great deal of knowledge has been developed regarding what works and what doesn't work in social services.

GPRA: Unintended consequences

- GPRA's use of the term "performance measurement" obscures the fact that far more than measurement is needed for performance *management* (as will become clear in what follows).
- A naïve focus on evaluation has led to many inappropriate and/or premature studies, with the alarming discovery that most programs don't work. This has fueled cynicism regarding what the government can accomplish.

- Demand for instant evaluative information leads to bad policies based on preliminary findings. For example, in the case of the U.S. government's $4 billion 21st Century Learning Centers program, one year's worth of evaluation data was used as the basis for arguing that the program should be cut by $1 billion. Although the George W. Bush administration was forced to reverse this decision because of massive lobbying efforts by social service advocates, the reasoning of the advocates was troubling and amounted to a Luddite assault on the relevance of evaluation in the social sector per se—as opposed to an argument for a more reasonable approach to evaluation and its use.
- Unfunded mandates for local performance—lack of investing in local capacity to manage performance robustly—results in the creation of disempowered local agencies and cynicism about government bureaucracy.
- Centralized implementation leads to clumsy, top-down decisions that engender data corruption, blame, and the politicization of what should be local efforts to "fix" what isn't performing well. Consider a notorious example, the decade-old No Child Left Behind (NCLB) legislation. NCLB was bipartisan and driven by a very legitimate desire to improve schools and student performance across the country, and especially in its revised iteration as the Obama administration's "Race to the Top" legislation, it has shown notable successes. Yet these laws also have resulted in awful unintended consequences—such as corruption by teachers and school administrators who have altered student answers and scores on mandated standardized tests, and at times ruthless "reconstitutions" of schools that amounted to rearranging the deck chairs on the *Titanic* rather than doing something constructive to get the ship safely to port—that is, to improve local schools' capacity to educate children.

In January 2011 the U.S. Congress updated GPRA by passing the Government Performance and Results Modernization Act 2010

(GPRMA). While the GPRMA legislation renews GPRA's reliance on measurement and evaluation, *it extends its scope to include the requirement that agencies must articulate operational frameworks and plans for monitoring performance.* This is a very notable step beyond GPRA, which referenced performance management in only the most general of terms.

In addition to Congressional action, the U.S. Office of Management and Budget (OMB) has played a key role in advancing the use of evidence as a basis for policy development and funding decisions. In 2004 OMB specified the use of randomized control trial (RCT) evaluation methods as the preferred way to produce evidence concerning government programs—that is, as the preferred approach for federal departments and the programs and organizations they support to show that they are in fact getting results as intended under GPRA/GPRMA. This well-intentioned wish for scientific rigor as the basis for establishing "what works" (and, as a corollary, "what doesn't work") has had its own unintended and indeed destructive consequences, as I will explain in Appendix I, a discussion of the relationship between evaluation and performance management.

═══

My hope is that in addition to its practical value, the book may also help to undo some of the negativity that has been a by-product of poorly implemented performance-management demands by government, foundations, and other funders. Those who rely on social services in order to overcome personal, economic, and societal challenges need the social sector to embrace performance management, to "manage to outcomes" with dedication, commitment, and passion. Yet failure by organizations in this sector to deliver promised results is well documented (see, e.g., Gueron 2005, Morino 2011). This is simply unacceptable because poor performance by social-sector organizations undercuts the initiative and hopes of their intended beneficiaries; it demoralizes those who are trying as hard as they can to better themselves and improve their lives; and ultimately it helps sustain social inequality here, in the richest country in the world.

CHAPTER 2

Why I Take Performance Management Personally

A period of my professional life that had an enormous impact on me came in my forties, when I helped turn around Cedarcrest Regional Hospital, an acute-care state psychiatric hospital in Newington, CT.

It was a time of struggle and more than occasional agony. From my current vantage point I can see clearly the embarrassing number of mistakes I made. I indulged a hair-trigger temper. I escalated to drastic solutions far too quickly. I failed to "walk in the shoes of others." I rarely turned to potential mentors for advice. In my defense, I can only plead youth—and an almost crushing sense of personal accountability for the lives of the patients who had been entrusted to my care.

The example I'm about to share is misleading in at least one way: It presents in a linear manner a transformation that in reality was a meandering process, consisting in fits (literally) and starts. The story suggests an upfront clarity that I didn't have, and efficiency in implementation that I couldn't even imagine.

When I took over leadership of the hospital in 1991, the concept of performance management had not yet emerged into widespread use, as far as I know. Certainly I didn't know anything about it. But perhaps because of my background as a social scientist, I did have a ferocious conviction that in order to make wise decisions we need to have robust, timely, and accurate information. That became the foundation of my efforts to lead the hospital's turnaround. And in the course of that work I learned about each of the pillars and elements of performance management that I will describe in detail in Chapter 3.

Here's my story.

At about 8:00 a.m. on November 1, 1991, I walked into the front hall of the acute-care state psychiatric hospital for which I had just been appointed superintendent (chief executive officer). Rather than head directly to my office, inspired by the then-voguish philosophy of "management by walking around," I detoured onto one of the five locked wards. Each held twenty patients who had been deemed a "danger to self or others" by a psychiatrist at a community hospital in the area.

Nobody challenged or even approached me as I entered. That was somewhat surprising, given that I was unknown to the hospital staff and that I was entering a ward full of patients officially labeled dangerous. As I stood near the door scanning the ward, my gaze was almost immediately captured by the sight of an elderly man sitting on the floor about twenty feet from me in what seemed to be a puddle of urine. He was rocking back and forth, occasionally hitting his head against the wall. And for five minutes, by my watch, nobody did anything.

Finally I approached the nursing station and asked the nurse behind the desk for the person in charge. She looked at me quizzically.

"What do you mean?" she said.

I was speechless for a moment, thinking that the question was pretty basic and absolutely essential to managing a ward for dangerous patients. So I pressed my question until she decided that the right person for me to talk to was most likely the "charge nurse." At no point did she ask me who I was or what my issue might be.

Eventually I was able to speak to the "charge nurse," and I asked her why the patient on the floor was not receiving any help. Her first response was to ask me who I was. (Finally!) When I told her I was the new director of the hospital, she took my question seriously. The nurses couldn't help the man, she explained, because the psychiatrist of record had not yet examined the patient, who had been brought to the unit within the past hour, and thus had not yet written any treatment orders.[2]

When I summoned the psychiatrist and asked why this was the case, he pointed to the fact that the social worker had not yet completed her admission paperwork, so he could not examine the patient. The social worker defended her performance by saying she had been having a series of unproductive telephone conversations with the referring hospital because the transfer information was incomplete.

I was already very disturbed by (even angry at) the lack of personal and professional responsibility. Yet a series of questions revealed an even more appalling fact. On the level of the ward, nobody was actually in charge! The psychiatrist reported to the chief of psychiatry, the social worker reported to the director of social work, the nurse reported to the director of nursing, and so on. All those chiefs of the various professional disciplines worked in offices away from this (or any) ward, and had no means to monitor whether or how the work was getting done on the ward, except in retrospect when they checked in.

This single experience—it can be thought of as a "sentinel event"—was enough to convince me that the hospital had a dysfunctional system and a culture in which performance expectations were set abysmally low.

An hour later I led my first executive-team meeting. It included all the aforementioned chiefs plus the director of rehabilitation services, the human resources director, and the director of finance and administration. After a brief get-acquainted chat, I told them what I had just experienced. Then I said, "We've absolutely got to have unit chiefs so that people can be held accountable at the point of service—the ward—for what they do and how they work."

2. This in itself failed to conform to a well-established practice in acute-care hospitals—namely, keeping two staff members within arm's reach of newly admitted patients until they have been assessed for their risk of dangerousness. It does not require a physician's orders if written into the hospital's "Policies and Procedures" manual.

The response around the table was not encouraging. In effect, the entire executive team agreed that (a) the hospital was unionized, (b) union contracts governed all operations, (c) there were no ward chief or unit chief jobs recognized by any of the contracts, and therefore (d) it was not possible to institute such positions to manage work at the ward level.

I looked around the table in disbelief and decided that this moment would either make or break my tenure as superintendent.

"So . . . we have turned over management of the hospital to the unions," I said.

I paused. Nobody said anything. So I continued.

"Here's what is going to happen. We are ending this meeting now. Tomorrow we will meet again at this time. There will be only one agenda item, namely how to implement a system of ward chiefs. Any one of you who doesn't have something to contribute to that conversation should not attend. And anybody who doesn't attend will not have a job, effective immediately."

Some people call what I did "creating a burning platform"—in this case for the executive managers.

Not me behaving well. Not a pleasant experience. But it worked.

The next day's meeting revealed that the hospital's management team could indeed manage the hospital. Further, the team could make decisions that were not anticipated by the union contracts—and even decisions that contravened specific contract provisions. Union members would have to comply with these decisions, but of course they could (and would be expected to) file grievances immediately. The grievance process, however, was far from efficient; as a rule, it played out over many months.

The team decided that although it would be incredibly challenging to deal with the multiple grievance processes they anticipated, it was worthwhile to work with me on a plan to appoint the five clinically strongest staff members who showed some interest in management to the new unit chief positions. The idea was to implement a simple management matrix: each unit chief, regardless of discipline, would be held accountable for managing the work flow of his or her ward, and hence could assign and monitor the completion of tasks by all staff. The chiefs of the professional disciplines (psychiatry, social work, and so on) would be held responsible for monitoring work quality and holding the staff in their respective disciplines accountable for meeting professional practice standards.

A good start, but not enough of a lever to motivate serious organizational change. So I proceeded, shortly thereafter, to create a burning platform for the staff, whose complacent approach to the quality and pace of their work was striking.

Until that time, whenever a community hospital emergency service wanted to transfer a patient to our hospital, they called the "Admissions Office"—which I enclose in quotes because really that office functioned as a Barrier-to-Admissions Office. Its standard line was "Our beds are full; call back in a couple of days."

The beds *were* always full, in fact. No one seemed concerned about that, though surely it is not beside the point to note that it takes less effort to hold on to old patients one knows than to admit new patients one doesn't yet know. But the critical issue, as I saw it, was that patients who were desperately in need of care were being kept in restraints or in close to comatose conditions in community hospital emergency departments for two to three days at a time because our hospital was a bottleneck. Here was such abysmal care that I simply could not tolerate business as usual.

So I called a meeting of the "admissions" nurses and told them that, for the foreseeable future, I was taking over their role and could be called upon day or night to approve admissions for any referrals to our hospital. "And by the way," I told them, "I plan to say the same thing every time: 'Please bring the patient over here immediately!'"

This led to a lot of head-shaking. "You can't do that," they said. "We're always full. We rarely have room to admit patients."

To which I responded, "Well, let's remember our mission. We are an acute-care hospital. If we don't have room to admit patients who need acute care, then we'll assemble beds from pieces in the basement and put them in the hallways, and if necessary in the doctors' and social workers' and psychologists' offices. But we will take patients immediately upon referral!"

Of course such a stance will be tested, and for a few days that is exactly what happened. I admitted referrals immediately, even though our beds and rooms were full. Staff members—and, for that matter, managers too—became uneasy, then concerned, and finally panicked. They said we were creating a dangerous situation in the hospital, and if an inspector were to appear, we might be decertified and closed down.[3]

"Yes," I agreed. "We probably would. And should. How about we work together to run the hospital differently, so that we always have room?"

This was asking a lot of them, so to sweeten the deal I asked them to meet with their union representatives and come up with the most difficult, most problematic aspect of working in the hospital, and I would make a commitment to alleviating that problem. It didn't take long for them to identify as their biggest work issue the fact that there was a very high rate of violence among the patients. A large number of nursing staff were being injured, some seriously, and having to stay home to recover.

So I made the following offer: I would guarantee that we would drive down the rate of violence by 75 percent over the coming twelve months if they would do two things: (a) drop their grievances regarding the installation of unit chiefs, and (b) change the loose way in which we were using the American Psychiatric Association's scale for rating psychiatric dysfunction—the Global Assessment of Functioning (GAF) scale—and implement it rigorously, assessing every patient every day. Finally, I made an absolute commitment to resign

3. The hospital had received very poor ratings from both the Joint Commission on Accreditation of Healthcare Organizations (JCAHO) and the Health Care Financing Administration (HCFA), which approves federal revenues to reimburse the states for the costs of hospitalizing disabled patients. Closure of the hospital was an active item on the state government agenda before I arrived—a fact that the hospital leaders, managers, and staff had avoided acknowledging.

my position after twelve months if they went along with these requests and the rate of violence did not drop by the full 75 percent.[4]

This combination of "setting operational fires" plus a commitment to deliver a change that the staff wanted bought us twelve months of staff buy-in to the approach to performance management I was introducing piecemeal. During this period I was fortunate to be able to hire Roger Coleman, MD, MPH, as the new medical director. Dr. Coleman brought a very strong background in performance measurement and analysis. I also discovered that the director of nursing, Helene Vartelas, APRN, had long been dismayed by how low the performance bar had been set and had been yearning for the hospital CEO to support her ideas about how to improve patient care. Coleman and Vartelas effectively became co-chief operating officers of the hospital—a relentless "dynamic duo" if ever there was one. We soon became a very strong and determined leadership team, and things began to change.

1. We started the process of having every patient rated according to the GAF daily, and we made sure patients got to a rating of 65 before we discharged them. **This single measurement was the key metric for driving subsequent hospital improvements.** The GAF provided a simple measurement, easy to understand and easy to use, of what we adopted as our mission-determined intermediate outcome (a rating of 65 upon discharge for every patient). It also became the tool for monitoring our patients' progress daily. And under Dr. Coleman we began convening "crisis meetings" for all patients who did not move up in their GAF scores for three straight days. In these meetings we changed the practice of asking "What's wrong with the patient?" to "What aren't we doing that we should be doing, or what do we need to do better, for this patient?"
2. These crisis meetings identified key treatment gaps. In fact, we were providing about five hours of active treatment per

4. It would seem that I thereby created a burning platform for myself. But I already had such a burning platform as a condition of my appointment: I had been charged to eliminate the deficit and bring the hospital into the black.

week to each patient, a level way below national standards. We adopted the government's standard of twenty-five hours of active treatment per patient each week,[5] discovered that there were key competencies that many clinical staff members lacked (such as the ability to conduct psychoeducational groups on the wards, as opposed to one-on-one individual treatment sessions conducted in the professionals' offices). The director of medicine and the director of nursing set about training staff to work in these and other new ways. For example, when we discovered that we had a large subgroup of often violent or otherwise disruptive patients who were not psychotic but functioned as if they were (with diagnoses such as borderline personality disorder), we reviewed the literature and found a rigorously tested approach to working with such patients, called Dialectical Behavior Therapy.[6] Even though the hospital's budget was always in danger of slipping into the red, we made an upfront investment in capacity building and sent a dozen staff to be trained by the person who had developed DBT, Marsha M. Linehan, PhD, a psychology researcher at the University of Washington. Further, we tapped into the interests of a staff psychologist who was delighted to take over the delivery of DBT in the hospital (without expecting extra pay), and we arranged for the newly appointed DBT director and staff to receive ongoing case consultation and clinical supervision through Dr. Linehan.

3. By redesigning the hospital's clinical work to include more group-based, reality-focused treatment that emphasized evidence-based methods to manage symptoms and dysfunctional behavior, we were able to reach our target of providing twenty-five hours of active treatment to each patient every week—and the treatment we provided was better designed to help patients cope. Not surprisingly, patients began to get better more quickly, and the average length of stay at the hospital dropped from over 45 days to about 17.5 days per

5. The HCFA has this standard.
6. This form of treatment combines cognitive-behavioral techniques with methods for stress reduction and stress management.

stay. Further, contrary to the predictions by those staff who resisted the changes we were making, the average time that discharged patients spent in the community before returning did not drop; rather, it increased by some 50 percent—and that became the long-term outcome for which we held the hospital accountable. This was a **highly relevant long-term outcome for our target population**—chronically ill individuals with serious psychiatric disorders that periodically flared up in acute episodes, during which they became dangerous to themselves or other people.

4. Using the newly instituted daily patient GAF scores, we found that fully 20 percent of our patients were well enough that they did not need to be locked up twenty-four hours a day in order for us to manage their risk. Under the leadership of the director of social work and with the full support of the medical director and the director of nursing, we unlocked one ward and replaced it with a day hospital program (with associated residential beds). This program focused on community reentry through skill-building groups that prepared patients for leaving (which the social work staff loved). For example, eligible patients took trial trips out of the hospital into normal community environments (such as the mall or relatives' homes), including overnight community stays when appropriate. This led to a new system of managing patient flow in the hospital, with both patients and staff seeing a patient's transition to the new program as important evidence of his or her progress. Not only did this help reduce the time patients spent in the hospital (driving outcome achievement), it also saved a considerable amount of money, because the new program required fewer licensed clinical staff members to conform to regulatory standards (driving budget requirements).

5. Finally, under the leadership of Dr. Coleman and with full engagement on the part of the director of nursing, Helene Vartelas, and Margaret Higgins, RN, the quality assurance director, we initiated a **pilot project to drive down the level**

of violence among patients. We involved union representatives in the selection of staff to participate in planning the project and thereby secured buy-in from the start. The project entailed the following steps:[7]

a. **Data collection.** We tracked all incidents of violence over a three-month period.

b. **Data analysis.** We identified the contexts and conditions in which episodes of violence took place, and we searched for patterns.

c. **Accountability.** Through our data analysis we came to see that we needed to put in place a system of accountability for making decisions to increase patient freedoms (such as going to the bathroom unaccompanied). We agreed that on every shift one nurse would be the designated person to make such decisions on each ward, and that the treating psychiatrist would then review those decisions.

d. **Research.** We asked union members to immerse themselves in the literature about predicting violence among psychiatric patients and develop a list of the indicators that had been used in evidence-based studies of patient violence.

e. **Measurement.** The research team led discussions with other participants to distill the list of indicators down to a manageable dozen, and designed a rating tool using these indicators. We then began a series of training sessions in which nurses and psychiatrists used the tool to rate patients being considered for advancement to greater freedoms. Over time we worked to achieve "inter-rater reliability"—that is, ratings that were highly consistent from one staff member to the next.

f. **Organizational learning and performance management.** We required, after a pre-established date, the use of the rating tool before a patient could be advanced to a higher level of freedom. But we did not make the staff use the rating tool mechanically, because we did not want it to be used to override or subvert their clinical judgment. Of course we wanted to avoid making overly permissive decisions that granted freedoms too quickly. Just as important, though, was to avoid making overly conservative decisions that held back patient progress. We used the data we collected to learn from our experiences, and

7. The pilot project is described in Coleman and Hunter 1995; Coleman, Hunter, Vartelas, and Higgins 1996.

> rather quickly our staff got quite adept not only at using the tool but also—and more crucially—at making solid clinical decisions. Within a year of the introduction of the pilot project, our measurements showed a decrease in violence by about 80 percent—well above the 75 percent I had promised the staff. This was an all-around win: for patients, who avoided the trauma of becoming violent; for staff, who were getting hurt much less frequently; and for me, because by delivering on my promise I could keep my job.

In summary, over a five-year period we turned around a rather dysfunctional hospital that had been threatened with loss of accreditation by the JCAHO[8] and with decertification by the HCFA,[9] and developed it into a high-performing hospital where patients got well quicker, violence was reduced, and treatment met national standards. In 1996 the hospital was accredited "with commendation" by the JCAHO, which put it into the top 5 percent of all hospitals in the United States. The hospital culture had come to fully embrace high performance expectations.

I have shared this extended example in the hope that both its details and the conceptual framework that I subsequently developed out of these experiences will inspire and guide leaders to drive, and staff to embrace, needed organizational changes more intentionally, directly, and efficiently than we did. Table 1 summarizes the major elements of this case.

---

8. The Joint Commission on Accreditation of Health Care Organizations is a nonprofit agency to which the government cedes much of its regulatory assessment of healthcare organizations' performance.
9. The Health Care Financing Administration approves the reimbursement to states for the costs of treating people with disabilities.

Table 1. The Tangible Impact of Performance Management at the Psychiatric Hospital

ORGANIZATIONAL ELEMENTS	BEFORE NOVEMBER 1, 1991	AFTER OCTOBER 31, 1996
Operational metrics		
a. Average (mean) emergency room waiting time	2–3 days	1–2 hours
b. Average patient length of stay	45+ days	17.5 days
c. Level of patient violence	High (400 hours per month of patients in seclusion and/or restraint, which was our proxy for level of violence)	80% lower (80 hours per month of patients in seclusion and/or restraint)
d. Dosage of active treatment	Low: 5 hours per patient per week	400% increase: 25 hours of active treatment per patient per week
Patient outcomes at discharge (intermediate outcome)	Unclear or idiosyncratic to the treating psychiatrist	Patients achieve a rating of 65 or better on the American Psychiatric Association's Global Assessment of Functioning (GAF) scale
Hospital design	Five locked wards for all patients for the duration of their stays featuring patient security management	Four locked wards plus a new open ward/day hospital featuring treatment focused on community reentry—with planned patient flow moving from the locked wards through the open ward/day hospital
Staff competencies	All psychiatric treatment staff (psychiatrists, nurses, social workers, psychologists) have general mental-health training appropriate to their specialties	20% of psychiatric treatment staff (psychiatrists, nurses, social workers, psychologists) are trained in Dialectical Behavior Therapy (DBT) designed to treat a particularly challenging subgroup of patients
Certification by the Joint Commission on Accreditation of Healthcare Organizations (JCAHO)	At risk	Certification "with commendation," a rating that places the hospital in the top 5% of all U.S. hospitals
Accreditation by the Health Care Financing Administration (HCFA)	At risk	All risk elements fully addressed

CHAPTER 3

The Pillars of Performance

Organizations do not emerge full blown and high performing. It takes years of thoughtful design, capacity building, and program implementation for an agency to know its work thoroughly enough, learn from its efforts, understand its strengths and weaknesses, and refine its strategy to the point where it has a robust framework and platform for managing its performance. Over this period of time, it should focus on what I think of as the three pillars and six elements that support performance management.

Table 2. The Pillars and Elements of Performance Management (Hunter and Bohni Nielsen 2013)

PERFORMANCE MANAGEMENT					
PILLAR 1 PERFORMANCE LEADERSHIP		PILLAR 2 MANAGEMENT SYSTEM		PILLAR 3 INFORMATION AND KNOWLEDGE PRODUCTION	
Element 1: Operational Leaders—individuals who inspire commitment to organizational goals and objectives, and dissatisfaction with failure to achieve them	**Element 2: Operational Managers**—individuals who organize work with a relentless focus on maintaining high quality and the achievement of targeted results	**Element 1: Accountability Systems,** where front-line workers are assessed on their ability to achieve targeted results, and managers on the success of front-line staff	**Element 2: Results-Focused Budgeting** to deploy resources to build and sustain the organization's capacity to achieve targeted results	**Element 1: Measuring and Monitoring Systems** to learn from the work, support real-time adjustments, adapt to emergent conditions	**Element 2: External Evaluation** to support strategic decision making **Formative evaluations** to ascertain what actually is being done and how, and **summative evaluations** to determine what is being accomplished, and why or how

Pillar 1: Performance Leadership

Currently there is a lot of interest in entrepreneurship, which is often considered the same thing as leadership. This way of thinking focuses on the role of leaders in driving innovation and/or scaling up (extending the reach of) organizations. In this vein, leadership is often described as a charismatic quality. But performance leadership is broader, and it requires two elements: operational leaders and operational managers.

Element 1: Operational Leaders

Operational leaders are driven, with a strong sense of purpose and the ability to inspire others to follow the course they chart. But there is another side to leadership. Operational leaders relentlessly challenge the people around them. Thus they are intentionally disruptive within the organizations they steer. A leader never stops asking how well the organization is doing, never stops seeking information about organizational performance. While it is essential for a leader to mobilize commitment to high performance at all levels of an organization, it is equally essential for leaders to stimulate "performance anxiety" and drive concerns about the status quo downward through the organization.

Good leaders are uncompromising on issues such as service quality and the achievement of results. Their attitude is that the organization should—and will—do "whatever it takes"[10] to ensure that service recipients benefit as intended.[11] One way or another, performance leaders must demand, as Mario Morino bluntly put it in *Leap of Reason*, "Catch the vision or catch the bus!"

---

10. With a bow to Paul Tough's *Whatever It Takes: Geoffrey Canada's Quest to Change Harlem and America* (New York: Mariner Books, Houghton Mifflin Harcourt, 2009, first published 2008).

11. I have had the privilege of working closely with some astonishingly effective, results-focused leaders of nonprofit agencies. These include, to name only a few, Molly Baldwin of Roca, Inc. (Chelsea and Springfield, MA); Patrick Lawler of Youth Villages (headquartered in Memphis, TN, now operating in a dozen states counting the District of Columbia); Mindy Tarlow of the Center for Employment Opportunities (headquartered in New York City, now operating in three states and seven jurisdictions) Ginny Deerin and Bridget Laird of WINGS for kids (headquartered in Charleston, SC); Bob Rath of Our Piece of the Pie (Hartford, CT); Richard Buery of the Children's Aid Society (New York City); Sam Cobbs of First Place for Youth (headquartered in Oakland, CA); Tony Hopson of Self Enhancement, Inc. (Portland, OR); Nick Torres, former President of Congreso de Latinos Unidos (Philadelphia); Lynn Peters and Kourou Pich of HarborCOV (Boston); Mark Lieberman of Family Services of Montgomery County (headquartered in Eagleville, PA); and Lise Willer, director of Social Services in Esbjerg, Denmark. All embody the qualities described in this paragraph.

Leaders focus on driving strategic performance. The focus on tactical performance management is delegated to managers.

Element 2: Operational Managers

In contrast to leadership, the role of management is to be supportive—but with great expectations regarding what the staff can accomplish. Where leaders create anxiety, managers must channel it into productive work conforming to high standards. A manager's job is to deploy appropriate resources (funds, materials, information) toward operations in order to sustain excellence, nurture staff development in individualized ways targeted to improving those competencies that affect performance, and encourage incremental improvements in performance by individuals and in aggregate—with celebrations for successes small and large. But while managers will and indeed should empathize with the work challenges of the staff, it is essential for managers not to join "underground" complaining about leaders' incessant demands for improvement. Rather, strong managers align with the organizational imperatives articulated by leaders—or, when disagreeing in a given instance, communicate this privately to the leaders along with suggestions on how to deal with the matter.[12] And, of course, it is managers who implement and drive the organization's accountability system. Advice for performance managers could be: "Keep your focus on the charted course, your eye on the compass, your hand on the tiller, and your attention on what lies in front of you. Get the boat to the right port safely and on time."

High-performing organizations need both leaders and managers. Too many leaders without the counterbalance of managers will drive an organization into chaos. On the other hand, too many managers operating without leadership do little more than perpetuate the status quo. As the aphorism has it, the only way to coast is downhill. It is not easy—though it is essential—for organizations with a

12. It is probably harder to be an effective performance manager than a performance leader. At least it is more complex. Some fabulous managers with whom I have been honored to work—who are relentless in their focus on the quality and effectiveness of daily performance—include Brad Dudding of the Center for Employment Opportunities (New York); Lee Rone of Youth Villages (Memphis, TN); Anisha Chablani of Roca, Inc. (Massachusetts); Hector Rivera of Our Piece of the Pie (Hartford, CT); and Dominique Bernardo of Congreso de Latinos Unidos (Philadelphia).

commitment to high performance to have leaders in positions that drive strategy and managers in positions that drive operations.

Pillar 2: Management System

Neither leaders nor managers can function adequately without policies, procedures, and processes—that is, a management system to provide an operational framework and the levers to pull so that work gets done right. For the purpose of supporting performance management, two elements of management structure are worth emphasizing: accountability systems and results-focused budgeting.

Element 1: Accountability Systems

What does it mean for an organization and its staff to be accountable? Simply put, it means that the organization (a) gives each employee the means for assessing how well he or she is performing in relation to both the quality of work and the results the organization expects, (b) supports staff members[13] in bringing their efforts to a level that meets the organization's standards of excellence, (c) helps employees who fall short to diagnose why, (d) provides staff with individualized development opportunities to improve performance-related competencies, (e) if necessary, brings added resources to bear so staff can better meet performance standards . . . and, when all else fails, (f) discharges those staff (including managers) who, after receiving all this support, cannot bring themselves up to snuff. Such an approach to accountability requires:

- *Clarity* about what the organization is working to accomplish and what is expected from employees in each job position
- *Transparency* regarding performance expectations for all employees[14]

13. This includes volunteers whenever they are used in critical areas. High-performing organizations manage volunteers' work as if they were paid staff—at least with regard to the quality and effectiveness of their efforts.
14. Some organizations take transparency even farther, sharing actual staff performance data. The Center for Employment Opportunities posts such data internally, every month.

- *Human resource practices* that support accountability for high performance
- *Monitoring* of a few key variables that define success at the level of individual staff members and, in aggregate, for programs, divisions, and the organization as a whole

It can be tempting for leaders to push for top-down, command-and-control accountability systems. And in the short run, especially in times of great organizational stress—such as to work through a crisis, uncover fraud, or head off financial ruin—top-down control may in fact be necessary. But this is not what performance management ultimately is about. It is a matter of creating the conditions where basic operating parameters are designed so that work drives the organization's strategic interests—so that work optimizes the organization's ability to achieve its goals and meet its objectives. Once these are established, systems, supports, and processes must be put in place that will enable front-line staff and their supervisors and managers to work creatively and bring personal expertise to bear in ways that are guided by these parameters (and evaluated in terms of them). This is a matter of tactical management.

The merits of such "guided self-management" are well articulated by Atul Gawande (2009: 79) when discussing the utility of carefully designed, intelligently implemented checklists to drive successful surgery:

> *The real lesson is that under circumstances of true complexity—where the knowledge required exceeds that of any individual and unpredictability reigns—efforts to dictate every step from the center will fail. People need room to act and adapt. Yet they cannot succeed as isolated individuals, either—that is anarchy. Instead, they require a seemingly contradictory mix of freedom and expectation—expectation to coordinate, for example, and to measure progress toward common goals.*

Element 2: Budgeting for Results (Outcome-Based Budgeting)

I will leave the technical tasks of budgeting and financial management to appropriately trained experts. But from a performance-management perspective, budgeting in the nonprofit sector often falls short in two ways: failure to budget in a front-loaded manner for significant capacity-building costs, and failure to distinguish growth capital needs from operating revenue needs.

Failure to budget for capacity building. Since the vagaries of funding bedevil nonprofit organizations from the moment of their inception, a common solution is to launch them on a shoestring budget that is inadequate to support the capacity building needed for high performance. Things like performance-management data systems and even staff training are often put onto wish lists that will be made real "when we get funding." Unfortunately, wishing can go on forever, and consequently many nonprofits work hard and long to deliver value to intended beneficiaries without the full array of systems, process, competencies, and facilities it would take to do so reliably and sustainably. Sadly, many funders are only too happy to perpetuate this situation by making targeted, program-only grants.

Failure to separate growth capital needs from operating revenues. The matter of growth capital is not well understood in the nonprofit sector. The frequent failure to budget adequately for this is a particular instance of failure in up-front capacity building that emerges as a critical obstacle to success when an organization seeks to grow or extend its reach through methods such as replicating sites or franchising. Such scaling-up requires more than simply increasing operating revenues in parallel with growing service volume. It also requires very significant building of new capacities and competencies in the central headquarters and the assurance that new entities will have adequate resources and the right capacities from the moment their doors open.[15] Unfortunately, funders (who should know better) frequently are complicit in faulty budgeting. They often drive scale-up ventures by making grants that pay for the unit-based cost of expanded program capacity (increasing the number of people served) but do not cover the many additional costs that are inherent to building a larger organization and managing it well (Miller 2005).

In contrast, outcome-based budgeting links allocations not only to building and sustaining operational capacities but also to maintaining the production chain that leads to intended (and measurable) outcomes.

Pillar 3: Information and Knowledge Production

Few beyond the occasional Luddite would dispute the assertion that if an organization does not collect key information about operational functioning, it cannot manage its performance effectively, reliably, sustainably, and accountably. **The issue for performance management is not whether to collect data; it is which data to collect—and then how to convert performance data into actionable information to support both tactical and strategic decision making.** There are two main sources of organizational knowledge production: measuring and monitoring systems, and evaluation.

Element 1: Measuring and Monitoring Systems

Ah, the need to measure. Anybody familiar with the nonprofit sector has heard the pervasive complaint that direct-service agencies are being forced by their funders to collect reams of data. There is more than some truth to this narrative: nonprofits are indeed "drowning in a sea of data."[16] Data they collect frantically, often resentfully, and use mostly to satisfy their diverse funders.[17] Data they feed into funders' databases, mold into reports whose formats are predetermined by

15. There are some nonprofits that have made this distinction and in fact do invest up front in growth costs. These include Youth Villages and the Nurse-Family Partnership.

16. Snibbe 2006.

17. Each of which may well require the collection of unique data sets, and require that they be reported in dedicated databases that are of no use at all to the reporting nonprofit for managing its own performance.

funders, and massage into long applications for grants. Data that do not help nonprofits manage their own operations.[18] And it is undeniable that such frantic measuring to feed many masters creates a drag on nonprofits, often to the point of hampering their ability to do the work that is at the core of their missions.

But this fact does not lead to the conclusion that nonprofits shouldn't measure performance. The question is not *whether* to measure; it is *what* to measure. And to answer this question, an organization must have a very clear, well-articulated framework: an operational blueprint that describes its strategic goals and objectives and provides the tactical parameters within which staff will work in order to drive the organization to success in achieving its mission. Such a blueprint for strategic success—also known as an "organizational theory of change"—must, among other things, list the essential variables that an agency will monitor to keep itself on course. The elements for a blueprint of this kind are discussed in detail below. For now, it is enough to point out that constructing an actionable blueprint requires an organization to understand its mission extremely well, give up sentimental ideas about what it would like to accomplish if the world were a better place, and have the discipline to focus (and focus and focus) on that for which it holds itself accountable.

Here, to put some meat on these bones, is a generic list of the kinds of things that a high-performing social service agency will most likely monitor (Hunter 2006a, 2006b):

a. Program enrollment criteria and their use

b. Program participation by enrolled participants (time, frequency, duration)

c. Program completion (and characteristics of those who fail to complete a program)

d. Essential indicators of program quality

18. There is indeed reason to complain of funders' practices in this regard. Few funders are considerate of grantees when it comes to imposing transaction costs—and this at the same time that funders tend to resist paying even close to the costs of the management overhead needed to drive high organizational performance. But this explanation, while true, is not an acceptable reason for nonprofits to reject the need to collect critical data in order to drive organizational performance. Performance-management consultants have a key role to play in helping nonprofits get over this hurdle.

e. Incremental progress on short-term outcomes for enrolled participants

f. Aggregated intermediate and long-term outcome data

It is worth highlighting the need for organizations to understand their work thoroughly so that they can limit data collection to only those items that will drive operations and support essential organizational learning. The need is for a disciplined focus on data collection. This kind of focus has two drivers: first, every item added to the data collection system brings new expense—the costs of measurement activities, analysis, conversion into usable information, and delivery of information to decision makers in a timely manner (Kusek and Rist 2004).[19] Second, the more things an organization measures, the less it can focus on operational essentials—the core of its work. The performance-management adage "Focus, focus, focus" is especially relevant to the collection of performance data.

IN FOCUS

Selecting Performance Indicators

The acronym "CREAM" provides a useful guide to the selection of performance indicators to monitor. Indicators should be:

- Clear (described in concrete, operational language)
- Relevant (tightly linked to essential variables that drive performance)
- Economical (affordable to measure)
- Adequate (sufficient for the collection of essential performance data)
- Monitorable (measurable within the capacities of the organization itself, not needing external evaluators)
(Kusek and Rist 2004:166ff)

19. Once again to state the obvious: The more an organization measures, the more unhelpful data it will generate and the more its operations will be gummed up by such activities. In performance measuring and monitoring, less is better. But it is not easy to identify the few essential things to measure—or the discipline to hold to them. Here it is worth resurrecting the military acronym KISS—for "Keep it simple, stupid." Performance data should be KISSable—and high-performing organizations will undertake the rigorous self-reflection necessary to design performance data sets that meet this joyful standard. One approach to doing so is the "theory of change" workshop described in Chapter 4.

All this talk of measurement is not meant to belittle the collection of inspirational stories by nonprofit agencies. Such stories can be a source of joy, pride, and motivation to organizations, their staff, their supporters, and even their clients. But stories cannot substitute for measurement. Standing alone, a story—no matter how inspirational—provides no insight into an agency's overall achievements. Does the success celebrated in the story represent a typical outcome for this organization, or is it an anomaly? Without measurement, we cannot know.

On the other hand, quantitative performance data alone don't provide the kind of contextual, nuanced information we need to understand how effectively an agency is working. For this we need external evaluation.

Element 2: External Evaluation

Definitions of evaluation are manifold and emphasize various dimensions and approaches. I won't enter into the myriad debates here. Instead, I will rely on the generally accepted (broad) view that evaluation entails the systematic assessment of an attempt to produce significant change through intentional actions. Thus the objectives of evaluations include determining whether implementation conforms with design standards, whether goals and objectives have been met, whether intended outcomes have been achieved, whether impact or contribution can be established, and how likely it is that the evaluated effort is sustainable.

It is useful to highlight two fundamentally different but highly complementary kinds of evaluations, formative and summative.

Formative Evaluations

Such evaluations are undertaken during the course of a project (or intervention, program, or initiative) and answer the following kinds of questions:

- What is the program model, and what are its constituent elements? Are all elements being held constant, or are some changing in response to emerging realities or experiences? And of these elements, which are more likely to be essential in producing intended outcomes?

- Is the project reaching the people it was designed to help?
- Are services being delivered as designed (with fidelity to the model)? At the specified levels of intensity (e.g., two hours per day), at the intended frequency (e.g., three times per week), for the expected duration (e.g., a full calendar year)?
- Is the project enrolling people who meet the participation criteria (target population)?
- Of those who are enrolled, are there any subgroups that benefit more than others? Less than others? If so, what seem to be the reasons?
- Are there some subgroups that fail to complete the protocol at higher rates than others? Reasons?
- What are the patterns of service utilization?
- What is the rate of achievement of short-term and intermediate outcomes? Long-term outcomes?
- Are some outcomes more likely to be achieved than others? If so, why?
- Given the number or people being served, how big an effect would the project have to have on participants for this to show up as a statistically significant outcome? (This is called doing a "power analysis"—the smaller the number of participants, the larger the effects have to be to show up as statistically significant outcomes.)

In general, while formative evaluations utilize internally generated performance data, they also rely on the independent collection of performance data as a means to check the validity and reliability of the internally generated data. Such evaluations are extremely important for learning about how a project has been implemented and how it is running, and they point to areas that need to be improved in order to increase the effectiveness of what is being done. While formative evaluations do not ultimately answer questions of causality or contribution to the achievement of outcomes, they are very useful for organizations that are serious about undertaking their work with integrity and dedication to doing whatever they need to do to ensure that participants in their services benefit as intended. Such evaluations should be undertaken by external evaluators who have the distance and objectivity to ask and answer hard questions that are very difficult to address rigorously in the hurly-burly of ongoing work.

Summative Evaluations

Such evaluations are undertaken after a project has been running reliably for a significant length of time with fidelity to the codified model. Summative evaluations answer the following kinds of questions:

- What is the codified program model?
- Was it delivered with fidelity to implementation standards?
- What are the characteristics of the people who have received services?
- What are the patterns of service utilization? What are the patterns of participants completing the project as intended?
- How many participants, and what percentage of participants, achieved short-term, intermediate, and long-term outcomes?
- What was the size of the effect for participants who reached intended outcomes (e.g., how many points did the rating of a child's literacy and numeracy improve)? What was the level of statistical significance for the achievement of each outcome (e.g., did it reach the "gold standard" of a degree of confidence of 95 percent)?[20]

20. "Degree of confidence" means the statistical probability that the observed changes are due to the project intervention as opposed to other causes, such as normal maturation, other life experiences, or participation in other activities. Evaluators accept a degree of confidence of 95 percent as the level at which the effectiveness of a given intervention has been established, although this is a matter of tradition and has no inherent value. In fact, that percentage means that one out of every twenty studies is probably wrong in its findings. This is why such program evaluations should be repeated at reasonable intervals, which hardly ever happens in the social sector. Often a single evaluation of a program is used to tout its effectiveness for years and even decades. A good example is the study of Big Brothers Big Sisters by Public/Private Ventures (Grossman and Tierney 1998), which to this day is cited as evidence that this mentoring program "works."

There is an enormous literature about the technical requirements for doing summative evaluations that meet professional practice standards. In general, it is fair to say that evaluators believe that only randomized control trial (RCT) evaluation strategies[21] can adequately establish causality with regard to a project's ability to produce outcomes for participants.[22] There is considerable resistance to RCT evaluations among nonprofit practitioners, some of it for justifiable reasons, some having more to do with an antipathy to importing "science" into a field that sees itself as one of "art." One common concern has to do with expense, and indeed RCT evaluations can be very costly. But they need not be so if they use public data sets to determine outcomes for both participants and members of control groups (Coalition for Evidence-Based Policy 2012).

Furthermore, it is not always necessary to prove causality beyond all doubt. Indeed, the government of Canada has relied on evaluations that allow for "contribution analysis" rather than nailing down causality—that is, establishing with a great deal of confidence that an intervention has indeed contributed to participants' achievement of outcomes as intended (Mayne 2001).[23]

A note of caution: It is a good idea to establish that a project is ready for a summative evaluation by first undertaking at least one formative evaluation and then making the tactical and strategic adjustments that are identified as essential to increase the likelihood that the effort will be effective.

21. This is where randomizing methods are used to place preapproved participants into the program being tested and into a control group; consequently both groups are composed of people whose demographic and baseline characteristics are the same. This method has the virtue of eliminating what is termed "selection bias" as an explanation for why and how much program participants benefit.

22. Outcomes that have been proven to be the result of a given program or intervention through the use of RCT evaluations are called "impacts" (Gueron 2005).

23. This is something that seems to have escaped the thinking of American foundations and other funders such as the United Way, which often impose unrealistic evaluation expectations on grantees that are not ready to undertake them and where RCT evaluations may not even be appropriate.

Steps for Establishing Program Contribution

In order to develop confidence that a given program is making a meaningful contribution to the achievement of specific outcomes, the following steps are essential:

- **Clarify and refine the chain of "if-then" assumptions that underlie the program or intervention.** This involves specifying the target population that is being served, the activities and other outputs provided by the program, the short-term outcomes leading to intermediate outcomes, and the long-term outcomes that are made more likely by the achievement of intermediate outcomes.
- **Look for opportunities to gather evidence of any kind that strengthens the linkages of these assumptions** (or undercuts them, which then requires rethinking of the program model). This may involve doing case studies, identifying relevant research or evaluations on similar programs or with regard to similar target populations.
- **Track program implementation.** Specifically, see if the program is being delivered with fidelity to the original design. (This is done by tracking implementation standards and managing against performance standards.)
- **Use multiple sources of evidence about how well the program is working.** At a minimum, track the following data:
    - Enrollment data—the demographic and baseline profiles of those enrolled in the program
    - Participation/service utilization data—the dosage that each of the enrolled participants is receiving, how often, and for how long
    - Program completion data—including the rates at which people drop out early or are dismissed before achieving targeted outcomes, and the reasons for these events
    - Short-term outcome data
    - Intermediate outcome data
    - Key staff and client anecdotes, especially those which illuminate issues of program access, early program departure, indicators of program quality (good and bad), and unanticipated consequences that might suggest a need to reconsider some program elements
- **Undertake formative evaluations periodically.**

- **At strategically relevant points, and if feasible, undertake a summative evaluation.**

  (Adapted from Mayne 2001: 16)

Finally, with regard to performance management, it is not a bad idea to subscribe to the simple mantra **“No stories without data—and no data without stories!”**

Some of these matters are discussed further in Chapter 5.

CHAPTER 4

How to Get Started: Four Days of Intense Introspection

It is never easy to manage organizational performance at high levels of quality and effectiveness over the long haul. It requires a clear vision of what one is trying to accomplish, the right organizational capacities, the resources to do what is necessary, and the tenacity to keep on course even when the going is rough. In other words, an organization that holds itself accountable for producing results must have a strategy for doing so and the commitment to stick with it.

With its origins in military thinking, a strategy requires an organization to have:

- **A clear mission** that articulates the domains within which it will work and the results it wants to achieve (and why)[24]
- **A long-range plan for succeeding,** with well-developed goals and measurable objectives

In the absence of a strategy, it is unlikely that an organization will know how to focus on what it is working to achieve, or have a collective commitment to getting key results. By definition, however, strategy is a "big picture" concept, much like the view one has while flying across the United States and looking down on major

24. This is often referred to as an organization's "value proposition" by social entrepreneurs and funders who use what has broadly been termed a "venture philanthropy" approach.

topographical features. *To get to strategic success, one also needs a framework for making it operational—doable and successful down on the ground where the "small picture" is immediate, must be dealt with as it changes, and requires constant focus, concentration, and intentionality of effort* (e.g., rotating crops, managing irrigation). Such a framework is provided by what is often called a "theory of change"—a conceptual structure that provides a bridge from strategy to operations and keeps operations dedicated to and aligned with strategic priorities and criteria for determining whether success has been achieved.

What Is a Theory of Change?

A theory of change is best thought of as an organization's blueprint for success. It is the guide whereby the organization structures its daily activities to achieve its strategic goals and objectives. It also provides the framework within which an organization can examine what works and what does not work within its own programming, and manage performance for continuous improvement (Hunter 2006a: 183).

To develop its theory of change, an agency must answer the sets of questions shown below within the governing limits provided by its mission, goals, and objectives.

IN FOCUS

An Exercise in Thinking About Basic "If-Then" Assumptions in a Real Program

If you are a direct-service provider, answer the following questions about one of your core programs.

If you are a funder, answer the following questions using what you know about a core program of one of your grantees.

If you are a consultant or a technical-assistance provider, answer the following questions using what you know about a core program of one of your client organizations.

1. What is the intended target population (as specified by demographic and baseline characteristics)?

2. What is the program model? (List specific elements including: What services should be delivered? What activities should be provided? What staff (or volunteer) competencies are needed to engage in this work with a high level of quality and effectiveness? What dosage of services and activities should program participants get? How often? For how long?)
3. How many people can the program serve at any given time (in ways that can be expected to produce intended outcomes)?
4. How is enrollment managed to ensure that program participants meet the intended profile(s)?
5. What is the program completion rate?
6. What are the reasons why participants are dismissed before they achieve targeted outcomes or why they leave prematurely?
7. What are the services and other activities performed or delivered by program staff (or volunteers)?
8. What are short-term outcomes that are tracked to show that clients are benefiting incrementally and in a timely way?
9. What are the outcomes that clients are expected to achieve before they leave the program? What number and percent do so?
10. What are the external constraints that might interfere with clients benefiting from the program as intended?
11. What external information is available to think about how to improve the program (e.g., new research on the target population, new evaluations of similar programs)?
12. What plans are there for making adjustments to address constraints or to build on new information?

Let's elaborate a bit on some of these questions.

Target Population(s)

Whom is the organization in business to serve so that it can measurably improve some aspect of their lives? (And the corollary: Whom should it not serve, or serve minimally with no accountability for results?)[25] Two major elements are used to define a target population:

a. **Demographic Characteristics.** These are the constant or very-slow-to-change qualities that define a group. They include: (a) date of birth; (b) ethnic/racial identity; (c) primary language; (d) gender; (e) place of residence; (f) family composition; and (g) socio-economic status (including use of public subsidies).

b. **Risk Indicators.** These are the more changeable qualities that are often the reason why a program elects to work with a population, and therefore are also the issues that the program tries to meliorate. They are often age-related and include such things as: (a) frailness and/or poor health or being at imminent risk for poor health (including mental health and related issues); (b) having demographic characteristics that themselves pose high risks to the viability of current living or life prospects—such as poverty, being a teenage parent (or the child of one), living in foster care, being a high school dropout, transitioning out of institutionalization, being homeless, lacking access to health care, having below-age-appropriate educational attainment (or dropout status); (c) being involved with a public system such as mental health and/or substance abuse services, juvenile or criminal justice, foster care or child welfare; and (d) lacking in basic life skills and competencies that support adaptive functioning.

It is essential that organizations understand both the demographic and risk factors of the people they are trying to help. No organization

25. Not all agencies—and not all programs within agencies—are in business to create outcomes (i.e., change people's lives or prospects for the better). Some are satisfied to deliver high-quality services without any concern for outcomes. Typically this is true of community resource centers, soup kitchens, and arts-type services. Nevertheless, effective management of such "output services" also requires an organizational theory of change to provide a framework for delivering them at high levels of quality and in a sustainable manner. The focus of this book, however, is on outcomes-producing programs.

can help all the people who need help, and therefore selecting the target population on which it will focus is absolutely essential—not only because the scope of needs is so large and far beyond what any organization could reasonably tackle, but also because different demographic and risk factors require particular prevention and intervention strategies and services for which specific organizational expertise and staff competencies are needed. Every organization must understand its "sweet spot" and focus its efforts on those matters for which it is best equipped to make a difference. This involves being selective about program enrollment—recruiting people with issues the organization can address, and excluding others.

Organizations often find that the challenge of specifying the target populations for enrollment into their core (outcome-producing) programs is gut-wrenching. Saying no to anyone cuts against the value system of many nonprofits. But it is essential that they realize that saying yes to everyone will ultimately mean that they will be less successful in helping anyone. They need to say no in order to say yes well.

One key issue is the matter of the severity of risk an organization can address successfully. Choosing to work with people at "very high risk"—people whose problems are overwhelming—is a noble endeavor, but doing it well requires very high levels of organizational capacity and staff competencies. When nonprofits take up this work (all too often, usually at the urging of funders) without the necessary capacities and competencies, they are not able to be of much help and indeed can inadvertently do harm. In contrast, serving people who are in pretty good shape takes much less work and can result in the appearance that the organization is producing terrific outcomes. This is called "skimming" or "creaming" and is also a frequent practice. The irony, of course, is that once one investigates whether these outstanding outcomes are actually the result of the organization's work or are simply changes that most likely would have come about anyway, the organization may seem to be of little value. Every social service organization has to find the right path in the space defined by these extremes and then exercise strategic and operational discipline in holding to it.

Outcomes

There is a lot of confusion regarding the concepts of outcomes and outputs in the social sector. Let's clarify. "Outputs" refers to the number and kinds of people served, activities performed, and items produced by an organization. Printing and distributing materials for HIV/AIDS prevention, serving food in a soup kitchen, coaching people who are seeking work—these are examples of outputs. "Outcomes," in contrast, refers to the desired changes that programs produce for target population members who are enrolled and participating in their services. Outcomes must:

a. **Be a measurable change in some aspect of the life of an individual, family, or group.** Generally speaking, social service organizations are seeking to produce changes in attitudes, knowledge, skills, behavior, social position attained (e.g., graduating from high school), or risk factors. If one cannot or does not measure these changes, one cannot be sure that they have occurred, and one cannot manage operations to produce them reliably. For the purpose of managing performance, **an unmeasured outcome is not an outcome!**

b. **Be relevant to the needs of the target population.** One does not select program outcomes in a vacuum; they have to make sense for the target population one is serving. To select good program outcomes one needs to have (or have access to) considerable knowledge about the target population and its needs. Looking to reduce violence committed by frail elderly people living alone, for example, is not likely to be a worthwhile endeavor. But not all such disconnections between target population and program outcomes are so obvious, and I have found that many organizations need considerable help bringing them into good alignment.

c. **Be sustained.** If an outcome is truly significant for a given target population, it must be sustained to make a worthwhile difference. A bit later I will distinguish among short-term, intermediate, and long-term (ultimate) outcomes. All three must be sustained to be important. If, for example, a high school student is at risk for dropping out, it makes sense to reduce his or her truancy rate, but the reduction is meaningless if school attendance is improved for only a week. It can be extremely useful to teach work-readiness skills to unemployed people looking for work—but only if they retain them. The same is true in the case of parenting skills for new parents, safe-sex practices for teens, self-care for people with chronic illness, pro-social attitudes for criminally involved youths and adults, and so on. Getting outcomes to "stick" is not easy. And when they don't, more than a few organizations blame the intended beneficiaries, ascribing to them such things as "a lack of motivation." Such attitudes can be a major impediment to high organizational performance, and must be challenged by any effective leader—or consultant.

d. Be linked to program efforts. At the very least, there should be a *commonsense association* between program activities and the outcomes they are meant to produce among intended beneficiaries. There will be a lot more to say about this below in the discussion of program codification. But for now I'll simply note that a lack of alignment between activities and outcomes is surprisingly widespread. There are tutoring programs intended to improve the academic performance of middle school students where the curriculum is written by high school students who themselves are barely literate; pregnancy-prevention programming using "abstinence-only" approaches that have been proven ineffective, and indeed can cause harm because they don't teach safe-sex practices and thus leave participants more vulnerable to acquiring sexually transmitted diseases; case management services provided by staff who have not been trained in appropriate interview methods or without documented knowledge of referral resources; workforce development programs that harangue participants to improve their attitudes without concurrently teaching them specific skills; and on and on.

While an organization may not be in a position to test the presumed linkage between its programming and its intended outcomes using sophisticated evaluation methods (about which there will be more below), at the very least it should make the assumptions about such linkages clear and track service provision by staff, as well as service utilization and incremental progress toward outcome achievement by clients.

e. **Be the basis for accountability.** It makes no sense to measure outcomes, or to monitor their achievement, if this information is not used to review what the organization is doing and how effective it is, and then to consider what it needs to improve. The performance of front-line staff should be judged on how successful they are in helping the people they are serving achieve key outcomes, and the performance of managers on how successful they are in improving the success of staff. Very few nonprofits have implemented results-based accountability. Rather, they focus on whether activities are delivered as intended. While evaluators are only too happy to assess outcomes whether or not they are the basis of organizational accountability, from a performance-management perspective this is a disaster. Absent accountability, little of worth gets done reliably.

It is essential that a theory of change ask and answer this question: What is the sequence of incremental changes that program participants should pass through as they progress toward achieving the intermediate and ultimate set of outcomes for which the organization or program holds itself accountable?

Programs/Services

All programs and services are outputs and should be designed to produce specific outcomes for target population members. A theory of change should answer all of the following: What should the agency's staff (or volunteers) be doing for or with those enrolled in its services (intended beneficiaries)? How much per day or week is sufficient, and how long should the program or service go on? Where should the programming or services be delivered (e.g., home-based, center-based), and what are the necessary competencies of those who deliver the programming or services, so that an organization can be confident that members of the target population will progress through the outcome sequence as intended?

In other words, an organization's theory of change provides the framework within which it will work, learn from its efforts, and make the necessary (timely) organizational and programmatic adjustments it needs to succeed in terms of its mission, goals, and objectives. A theory of change is thus broader than a program logic model, although the terms are often used interchangeably. "Program logic model" refers narrowly to cause-and-effect statements that specify a particular program's inputs (resources expended), outputs (activities performed and products produced), requisite staff competencies, and intended beneficiary outcomes.

Without a theory of change for making its strategy operational, an organization is unlikely to have effective plans for achieving results, may not have amassed the right resources to support its plans, and will not be able to organize and manage its efforts to achieve results—reliably, sustainably, effectively, efficiently, and at high levels of quality. Thus both a strategy and an aligned theory of change (blueprint for success) are necessary preconditions for driving to results (managing to outcomes). Without them, it is unlikely that an organization will generate much of anything in the way of meaningful social value.

Characteristics of a Robust Theory of Change

At a minimum, a theory of change should be:

- **meaningful** to its stakeholders
- **plausible** (conforming to common sense and the opinions of experts)
- **doable** within resource constraints
- **measurable and monitorable** (specifying the metrics that will be used to manage it)
- **operational** (providing a useful framework for managing organizational performance reliably, sustainably, and at high levels of quality and effectiveness)

Theory-of-Change Workshops

This section presents a workshop approach grounded in my three decades of leading and managing social service agencies, as well as helping other organizations develop practical theories of change. In my experience, these workshops require four days of highly focused work. They require deep, cellphones-off participation by a "vertically integrated" team representing all levels of the organization: the board of directors, executive director, COO and/or director of programs and other leaders, mid-level managers and program directors, and a representative sample of front-line staff and supervisors from all programs. Generally such a group will have a maximum of twenty-five participants—a large but still workable number.

For large organizations, it may be necessary to conduct this work in two stages—the first with a strategic focus for board members and the executive leadership team, the second for mid-level management and front-line staff organized around divisions or programs. If the sequence is broken into these two stages, the second must be built upon framework constraints developed in the first workshop, where, among other things, the organization's mission and goals, as well as long-term and intermediate outcomes, are established.

The facilitator should communicate to workshop participants that these workshops have three objectives:

1. To help the agency develop a **top-to-bottom consensus** on what each department, program, and person contributes to the value of what the organization produces
2. To create a **blueprint for the (re)design of the agency and its programs** to make it robust and sustainable and its work measurably effective
3. To **design the performance-management system** that the agency will use to keep its work at the highest levels of quality, effectiveness, and efficiency

The workshops should provide a venue within which it is safe for participants to have hard, searching conversations and to forge a consensus around key strategic and operational matters. Those who work at the upper levels of the organization are likely to hear things about work on the front lines that will surprise and perhaps worry them. For example, they might hear that staff enroll people into programs without observing central protocols; that enrollment records may not accurately reflect who receives services; that in the absence of rigorous supervision or systems of accountability, staff follow their inclinations in what they do and what they don't do for or with clients; that the performance data collected by staff are of no use to them whatsoever in doing their work; or that staff do not feel much of an obligation to record data accurately, completely, or in a timely manner. In turn, front-line staff may learn about management's concerns regarding service quality; threats to the organization's future; real (as opposed to imagined) contractual constraints on the work; or how the organization's growth plans depend on narrowing enrollment practices.

These conversations should be forward-looking. They should challenge the status quo and emphasize what the organization needs in order to be a high performer that delivers good social value to those it seeks to benefit and the stakeholders who support it. This is far from easy. It requires a facilitator to be creative in helping people step outside their comfort zones and the usual frameworks within which they work (such as their "home" programs) and consider the agency as a whole. It is important that the facilitator help the group gain a deep understanding of the various perspectives and experiences people bring to their work and to promote discussions in which the participants can develop a consensus on key questions such as:

1. **Why should the organization be in business?** This calls for an examination of mission, goals, and objectives.
2. **Who should constitute our target population?** And an associated question: Which are our core (outcomes-producing) programs, and which are supportive, recreational, or expressive services (producing outputs but not outcomes)?
3. **Whom should the agency engage as "service population"?**[26] And what should be the indicators used to make sure that we maintain high-quality programming for them?
4. **Who should "own" a case?** Who is responsible for the success of a case? Every case needs a point person who coordinates services, monitors progress, initiates service adjustments as warranted, and so on.
    - In the organization's programming, what constitutes a treatment or service team? Usually a case needs the work of several people, sometimes across multiple programs.
    - How are cross-program and external referrals managed?
5. **What basic assessments should be made?**
    - How is program enrollment managed? What information is used to establish enrollment eligibility? Does an enrollment assessment need to be developed, or does the one in current use need to be modified (and if so, how) to ensure that only appropriate participants are enrolled?

26. In this framework, target population members are why an agency is in business. Service population members are part of how it does business. Organizations generally find it almost impossible to serve target population members only. There are numerous reasons, including the presence of legacy programs; funder requirements; the need to maintain credibility and promote ease of access in local neighborhoods; and the desirability of having a broad base of support when engaging in advocacy. Whatever the reasons, however, organizations should try to keep the bulk of their resources focused on core operations intended to produce outcomes for target population members.

- Once clients are enrolled, should there be a universal *baseline assessment* to guide service planning? What data sets should it include?

6. **What is the process for converting a baseline assessment into a service plan?** Who should participate in such meetings? What data should be used?
7. **Which services should the agency offer to help clients achieve the targeted outcomes?** And which such services should be outsourced?
   - What is the specific nature of the activities, and what is the necessary dosage (frequency and duration)?
   - Who has been assigned the task of delivering each activity, and what is the professional competency profile of the person who does so?
   - Are the organization's programs designed well and resourced adequately to drive intended beneficiaries toward the achievement of intended outcomes?
8. **What are the short-term client outcomes?** These are the short-term results of staff members' immediate efforts that are necessary contributors to clients' success. How will the organization measure and monitor them? How will staff and managers use these data to adjust the organization's efforts on behalf of clients?
9. **What are the intermediate outcomes** that create the conditions for service recipients to achieve the **long-term outcomes** targeted by the organization?
10. **To what degree does the agency plan to track people after discharging them?** If it is making a long-term promise to clients, it must track them.
11. **What do we need to do to manage our performance?** What are the supervision and management structures and systems? What is the accountability system? What competencies are needed for each position in the organization? Does the agency in fact have people with the right competencies in each position—and where it doesn't, what is the plan to

correct this? Does the budget support such organizational improvements, or does it need to be adjusted?

12. **What should the organizational structure be?** That is, what structure would best support performance management?

One should expect moments of significant disagreement and even conflict in these discussions. This is hardly surprising, since tacit issues and disagreements that have simmered below the surface will bubble up once the norms of workplace conversation are even partly suspended by the facilitator's efforts to promote transparency. The facilitator must use such moments as opportunities to help the group work through the conflict and emerge on the other side with a newfound sense of its competence, coherence, and mutual respect—as well as a more widely shared line of sight to the organization's mission-critical goals and objectives.

Where the group cannot achieve consensus, the facilitator must ask the executive director to make a dispositive decision and give the reasons for doing so (acknowledging the contributions made by all participants to the discussion). If this is not feasible in the moment, the executive director should designate a workgroup to produce added necessary information (e.g., about benchmark data) and specify a process through which he or she will then reach a final decision—with a commitment to communicate the ultimate decision and the reasons for it to the entire organization. The facilitator should use all opportunities to promote such transparency of thinking and decision making in order to drive the organization's evolution to a higher level of development and performance.

The Sequence of Activities

There is an underlying logic to the sequence at a theory-of-change workshop. The idea is to start at the relatively high level of abstraction represented by an organization's mission statement. Using that as an initial way to focus and constrain the discussion, the facilitator then drives downward, level by level, through the increasingly concrete and increasingly constrained elements: goals, objectives, target population, outcomes, and activities. In this way, decisions at any given level create the framework for getting consensus on decisions at the next level down. The dynamic of this funneling process is hard to believe if one has not worked with it—but it creates possibilities for reaching hard decisions faster, and with greater buy-in from diverse participants, than anyone can imagine at the beginning of the four-day course of events.

I have outlined the workshop sequence below. My outline suggests that the workshop is a fully linear process, but in practice that is never the case. In the course of each day, the facilitator should recognize when the conversation is taking the group outside the constraints of earlier decisions. He or she should address this explicitly by asking whether the group wants to revisit the prior decision (and, if so, give them space to do so) or whether the participants simply need to be reminded that they had agreed to stay within a framework whose boundaries they are now crossing. Thus, while it is fine for the group to "circle back" to prior decisions when the discussion has helped them appreciate some of the implications of those decisions more completely, such circling back should not be allowed to stall the process. The loops should look more like a three-dimensional spiral than a flat circle.

There is one exception to the practice of allowing the occasional circling back: the facilitator must protect the decision that workshop participants reached in settling on the agency's mission statement. Efforts to revisit that first decision should be highly discouraged, with the facilitator emphasizing that this dynamic—the wish to circle back to the mission statement—reflects significant organizational disagreement and suggests pretty serious confusion about why the organization is in business and what it offers to the world. If the facilitator can't help the organization to quickly reaffirm its newly adopted mission statement, he or she must raise the question of whether the agency is ready to undertake the organizational changes necessary to become high performing—and if not, whether the workshop should be terminated. This will provoke a crisis, but frequently the crisis will lead to a very constructive group dynamic in which the organization's leadership grows, its management functions sharpen, and staff members deepen their understanding and commitment to the organization.

While the typical workshop entails four days of work, it is a good idea to break the days up, perhaps doing one day a week for three weeks or holding meetings on two contiguous days separated from the next set by a number of days or even a week or two. The pauses allow the organization to review internal documents, reanalyze performance data, or research specific items such as the literature on evidence-based programs. And for very large organizations the workshop may take more than four days.

Preparation for the Workshop

It is very important to get a baseline description of an organization's programs before the theory-of-change workshop begins. This has two purposes.

The first is to provide the organization an opportunity to engage in some focused reflection on its service approach, and to discover on its own where it can do better. Such reflection might be about, for example, ensuring that service recipients receive appropriate levels of service at appropriate intervals and for a long enough time, that activities are performed by staff or volunteers with the right competencies, or that intended beneficiaries are being helped to achieve the best outcomes appropriate to their life circumstances. All high-performing organizations engage in such stock-taking routinely. But agencies that are not yet there can benefit greatly from being offered the opportunity to engage in this kind of reflective exercise, stimulated rather than guided by the consultant, and thereby develop a new capacity or nurture a fledgling one. This is an important precursor to adopting, implementing, and institutionalizing strategic and tactical performance management.

The second purpose is to help the facilitator understand how well the organization has thought through its services and understands their strengths and weaknesses—and also to take note of possible "blind spots" where the organization is engaging in activities that are more or less simply carrying on what it has done for a long time without systematic reflection. This information will inform how the facilitator addresses the agency's practices. For example, the facilitator might determine that it's best to take an incremental approach that identifies ways the organization can improve on its programming; or, in contrast, he or she might see an opening to take a more radical approach in which fundamental programming assumptions can be challenged—an approach that will require helping the organization work through the cognitive dissonance that such a challenge will inevitably stimulate.

For these reasons, it is a good idea to ask program directors—well in advance of the workshop—to fill out some version of the worksheet in Appendix II, and to disseminate the completed worksheets to workshop participants and the consultant a week or two before the meetings begin.

Day One: Mission, Goals, Objectives, Populations

It is essential for the organization's leader (executive director, CEO) to open the workshop by welcoming participants and reminding them why the organization is going through this process, what it hopes to gain, and what the participants will need to do to ensure that the objectives are met. One especially important point to make is that the cost in salaried time for these meetings is high, and can only be justified if all participants are active and honest. This requires courage: a participant may have to express views that conflict with what someone at a higher level in the organization has put forward. But it is impossible to reach robust decisions unless information and opinions (even when they may be oppositional) are brought forward, considered thoughtfully, and acted on appropriately.

Since most workshop participants will not know all the others, it is important to hold a brief round of self-introductions, with participants noting what they, personally, hope will come out of the workshop. The facilitator should go last, mention relevant information about his or her background and experience, take note of the hopes that participants have expressed, indicate which seem likely to be met and which might not, and briefly outline the four-day sequence and what will be covered on each of the days. It is a good idea to signal that the work will most likely be draining, and that it will get progressively harder from Day One through Day Three, with Day Four generally less taxing.

Then, after the usual logistics—break times, meals, and so on—are settled, the work can commence.

During these workshops the facilitator should not assume that participants mean the same thing when they use the same words. This is especially true on this first day, when they are considering large issues such as strategic focus, mission, goals, and objectives. He or she should be alert for moments when what participants say need clarification.

The first day's work should proceed through the following sequence:

- ***Step 1: Review and clarify strategic decisions*** that the organization has made (e.g., to emphasize program improvement or to scale up operations), and improve its strategic focus where indicated. This should serve as the limiting framework for all subsequent discussion.
- ***Step 2: Clarify the agency's value proposition***—that is, its mission, goal(s), and objective(s). This day's discussion must start with the organization's statement of mission. It is fair to say that the mission statements of most nonprofit organizations are overblown fluff, meant to appeal to sentiment rather than convey a serious purpose. Often they are delusionally optimistic, promising change on a scale utterly out of proportion to the agency's resources or intervention efforts (e.g.,

proposing to create a "safe community" by providing after-school services). Here it is very useful for the facilitator to adopt a kind of "village idiot" stance ("I apologize in advance for my ignorance, but I'm going to ask a lot of questions to make sure I understand what you're saying"). The facilitator should constantly reflect back what she or he "hears" in order to help the group become clearer, more specific, and more realistic in its thinking.[27]

- ***Step 3: Define and codify the organization's target populations***—that is, the people whom it enrolls in its core services and to whom it holds itself accountable. These are the people mentioned in the organization's mission, who are thus the reason it is in business.

An Exercise in Mission Clarification

First, consider the following mission statements,[28] which are typical of many social-sector organizations:

Boys & Girls Clubs of America. Mission: "To enable all young people, especially those who need us most, to reach their full potential as productive, caring, responsible citizens."

COMMENT: Yes, but who are the individuals who need BGCA most? And is it realistic, even for an organization as large as BGCA, to enable all young people to reach their full potential? And can BGCA really claim that all of its local affiliates (independent, freestanding nonprofit agencies) work equally well to achieve this mission? In a nutshell: Can BGCA deliver on its mission? Seriously?

Healthy Families America. Mission: "Healthy Families America, a program of PCA America, strives to provide all expectant and new parents with the opportunity to receive the education and support they need at the time their baby is born."

COMMENT: "Strives"? That's it? Really? No problem if it fails to deliver? And by the way, providing an "opportunity to receive . . . education" is a far cry from actually educating people. And if participants are actually educated, to what end? Is there any meat in this sandwich?

27. Because of this imperative, I don't engage in "visioning" exercises with client organizations. In my view, there is far too much sentimental visioning going on among direct-service providers and funders—much to the detriment of the social sector and the people it is intended to help.
28. These are quoted from the organizations' websites.

Second, write down the mission of an organization you lead, manage, fund, or consult to:

Third, respond to the following questions by circling the appropriate answer:

1. Does the mission statement contain any terms that are vague, impressionistic, visionary, or wishful rather than specific and concrete?
   Yes No I'm not sure
2. Does the statement include terms that make sense to people who are part of the organization's milieu but perhaps don't carry much meaning for "outsiders"?
   Yes No I'm not sure
3. Does the mission reflect a "vision" or hope rather than a realistic set of assumptions and intentions?
   Yes No I'm not sure
4. Does the mission make clear why the organization exists, the domains within which it works, and what it seeks to accomplish? In other words, is the mission statement an articulation of the organization's *value proposition*?
   Yes No I'm not sure
5. Does the mission go beyond what the organization *does* and indicate what it wants to *accomplish*?
   Yes No I'm not sure

For questions 1–3, if your answer was "Yes" or "I'm not sure," try to provide alternative language that would lead to an unambiguous, affirmative version of the mission statement. Do the same for questions 4 and 5 if your answer was "No" or "I'm not sure."

Let's consider an example in a bit more depth.

Mission, Goals, and Objectives

The Children's Aid Society of New York City (CAS)[29] has a history—one that extends back more than one hundred years—of wanting to serve New York's children and their families in every conceivable way. To do so it has been running dozens of citywide and neighborhood-based programs in areas as diverse as health clinics, foster-care services, preschool programs, after-school programming, tutoring, mentoring, a summer camp, employment services, and more, earning appreciation from city government, neighborhood groups, and the families and individuals it serves.

29. The CAS material presented here was generated by a series of theory-of-change workshops that I facilitated; I have the permission of Richard Buery to share them.

When I began my work with CAS, its mission statement read:

> *The Children's Aid Society provides comprehensive support for children in need, from birth to young adulthood, and for their families, to fill the gaps between what children have and what they need to thrive.*

Here are some questions I had for the organization:

- But what are the gaps, and what does filling them entail?
- Can any one agency fill all gaps?
- Does CAS really propose to serve all the children in the city?
- Is CAS responsible not only for the children's outcomes but also for those of their families?

Recently, under its new president and CEO, the agency had come to recognize that it was not living up to its potential. As its new president and CEO Richard R. Buery Jr. observed on the first day of an extended series of theory-of-change workshops, the agency lacked focus—and specifically, it was not addressing what he believes is the most dominant fact of life confronting the children that CAS should be serving: poverty. As Mr. Buery put it:

> *Despite the good CAS does for tens of thousands of families, including the lives CAS has literally saved, we cannot say with certainty that the children who enter CAS programs will—as a result of our work—consistently become adults with the skills and education necessary to escape the poverty into which they were born (Buery 2011).*[30]

30. The remainder of the CAS case description relies on the same document.

After considerable discussion, debate, and introspection in the workshops, the group achieved consensus regarding a key strategic matter. In their words:

> *First, although the breadth and depth of CAS's services are inspiring, many of the services that we provide are short-term or limited to a specific aspect of a child's life. This is the result of structuring ourselves to meet the needs of public funders focused on short-term interventions, instead of organizing ourselves around the long-term, complex needs of our clients.*
>
> *Second, although staff will go to extraordinary lengths to assure the safety, health, and happiness of our children, not all of our programs have defined their intended outcomes or can track whether they are achieving them.*
>
> *Third, our organization operates in silos. The benefit of being a comprehensive multi-service agency is the opportunity to meet all of our clients' complex needs. Yet because our services are not fully integrated, it is not always easy for our clients to know what services we provide or how to access them. In addition, a teen who walks into one CAS center might receive a completely different service than he would receive at another site simply because the programs—which might operate in different divisions and with different priorities—do not share a common standard of success.*
>
> *As an organization, CAS recognizes that if we want to be more certain of the impact we are having in moving children out of poverty, we need to be more disciplined; client-centered rather than organized around funder mandates; and committed to articulating, measuring, and tracking the outcomes that will help children escape poverty and achieve life-long success. Our children deserve no less.*

These are courageous and crucial strategic insights. And they led CAS to ask **four key strategic questions**:

- **Which children are we here to serve?** (How do we define our target population? Where do they live? What are their demographic characteristics? What are the key risk factors that we look for?)
- **What outcomes do we want to achieve for the children we serve?** (What measurable and meaningful changes do we want to occur in children's lives as a direct result of our efforts?)
- **What services will we provide in order to achieve these outcomes?**
- **How must we change as an organization in order to achieve those outcomes?** (How will we create the programmatic and organizational structures required to drive consistent program quality and client outcomes?)

After considering these questions in depth, the group reached the following **four strategic decisions**:

1. The group adopted a revised, much tighter mission statement:

   The Children's Aid Society helps children in poverty to succeed and thrive.

   To which CAS added a clarification of the service approach it developed in these workshops:

   We do this by providing comprehensive supports to children and their families in targeted high-needs New York City neighborhoods.

2. Thus CAS drew back from providing citywide services, deciding instead to work with children living or going to school in specifically targeted, low-income, high-risk neighborhoods in New York City.

3. CAS adopted educational attainment as the mechanism to leverage these children out of poverty. Therefore, CAS created "outcome maps" (short-term, intermediate, and long-term outcomes) using educational process, performance, achievement, and attainment metrics to understand ongoing success and guide constant reassessment and "real time" (tactical) adjustments as indicated—at the level of each case, program, and division, and at the organizational level as well (although here decisions will of necessity be more strategic in nature).
4. Finally, CAS decided to implement uniform performance-management practices and data utilization across the entire agency.

The group understood that this required the agency to narrow its focus on poor children, declaring, "We are a poverty-fighting organization." Further, it led to the recognition that CAS would need to engage over long periods with every child it serves in order to help each one break out of poverty. And finally, CAS acknowledged its limitations and drastically narrowed its focus by deciding to work with fewer children (in just a few neighborhoods) in order to be able to work with them longer and more intensively—and thereby more effectively. That is, it adopted the strategic principle **"Children's Aid Society would rather transform the lives of a few than simply serve many."**

This is the kind of mission clarity, with consequent strategic specificity and focus, that is necessary for an organization to become high performing.

A clear and well-articulated mission provides the context within which the organization can specify its strategic goals. While the term "goals" has many definitions, from a performance-management perspective it is useful to define it simply:

> *Goals are statements of the criteria that an organization will use to judge whether it has been successful in achieving its mission at a specific point in the future.*

Practically speaking, it is wise to keep in mind that organizations proliferate goals as they lose strategic focus (often driven in this direction by their multiple funders). A good rule of thumb is to try to keep the organization committed to no more than five goals at any given time.

The term "objectives" also has many definitions, but in this context it is a relatively straightforward matter:

> *Objectives are the series of measurable milestones that an organization will use to monitor progress along the way to achieving each of its goals.*

Let's return to the example of CAS. Here are the four goals and the associated objectives that the leadership group adopted on its first workshop day.

Goal 1: CAS will build the organizational capacity and structure CAS needs to manage programs at high levels of quality and effectiveness.

Objectives:

- **a.** Organize the board to hold CAS accountable and raise needed resources.
- **b.** Design the organizational structure in alignment with desired outcomes—including both program services and infrastructure.
- **c.** Build a performance-management system that allows CAS to measure and report on outcomes and hold ourselves accountable for getting children to outcomes at each developmental level. This includes strategic planning capacity to drive changes required to improve outcomes; quality assurance and compliance; IT and data collection processes; and program evaluation.
- **d.** Increase the capacity of the back office—data systems, business functions, IT, communications.

e. Build human capital, including recruitment, retention, hiring, orientation, training, supervision, competency-based job descriptions, evaluation, and firing.

Goal 2: CAS will implement a neighborhood-based strategy.

Objectives:

a. Identify neighborhoods and conduct community needs assessments.[31]

b. Identify ideal array of services.

c. Identify effective interventions—consider approach, how to integrate, how to engage the community.

d. Conduct internal assessment of what we can/should do.

e. Identify community partners to complement what we can do.

f. Identify/get space in neighborhoods.

Goal 3: CAS will undertake advocacy to (1) change the policy framework in which children's services are delivered in NYC; (2) improve the environment under which CAS works; and (3) disseminate program models that improve the lives of poor children.

Objectives:

a. Create both proactive and reactive policy agendas based on mission and strategy. This includes creating policy targets, making this process an inclusive and strategic one, and seeking advisement from our clients.

b. Develop the internal capacity (trustees, staff, and clients) to be effective advocates.

c. Identify effective replication and dissemination strategies (conferences, discrete grants, testimony, etc.).

d. Identify and collaborate with prospective partners and coalitions. Identify gaps in coalitions where we should

31. This was done as part of the strategic planning process.

take the lead, including collaboration with politicians and policymakers.

- **e.** Develop an effective communications strategy on our agenda and proven practices; become the "go to" professionals on issues affecting our target population. This includes active dissemination of practices for programs we know are effective.
- **f.** Assess impact on broader policy and practice. (Identify our intentions and assess if they were achieved.) Integrate policy work throughout the work of the agency.

Goal 4: The Board of Trustees and management will work together to obtain the funding we need to support excellence, promote innovation, and to sustain core programs despite fluctuations in funding.

Objectives:

- **a.** Develop a coherent fundraising message.
- **b.** Review all assets including endowment and intellectual property and assess strategies for monetizing those assets (e.g., how much should we charge for technical assistance from the Stern Training Center?).
- **c.** Substantially increase giving from individuals (double from $6 million)—needed for sustainability of core programs during droughts in restricted funding, to fund innovation, advocacy, and our performance-management system.
- **d.** Trustees will raise private funding equal to 10 percent of public contracts.
- **e.** Emphasize different kinds of fundraising beyond traditional direct mail; branding, PR; focus on younger generation, use Associates Council, social media, etc.
- **f.** Maximize public funding opportunities through advocacy and strategic partnerships, and build the agency's capacity to transfer public funding responsibility from program staff to development staff.

Once the work on goals and objectives has been taken as far as possible within the context of Day One, the process should move on to the next step. (The work on objectives can be completed outside the workshop by a group designated by the organization's leader.)

Target and Service Populations

As noted above, to specify target populations one needs to identify both demographic and baseline indicators and make clear how these will be used to manage the enrollment of service recipients in core programming. Here we restate the definitions for emphasis, and we go a bit deeper.

Demographic indicators are qualities that are fixed, such as date of birth, ethnic/racial identity, primary language, gender; or that inherently tend to be slow to change, such as place of residence, family composition, and socioeconomic status. Demographic indicators generally define the context within which people live and function.

Risk-related indicators consist of aspects of people's lives that generally are malleable (though some may be slow to shift) and that the organization identifies as important to know about in order to serve its target population effectively. Risk-related indicators generally identify variables that pose likely impediments to adaptive functioning.

Two categories of risk-related indicators are generally very relevant:

- **Status factors.** These are similar to demographic indicators in that they tend not to change very quickly, but unlike demographic indicators they have well-established risk factors associated with them. Examples include:
  - Poverty
  - Unemployment or underemployment
  - Homelessness

- Chronic illness
- Family composition (e.g., a family with a teenage mother and no resident father, headed by a grandmother)
- Social isolation
- Living in unsafe conditions (either the housing or the neighborhood)
- Having an antisocial peer group
- Incarceration
- Being in—or aging out of—foster care
- Falling one or more grades behind in school
- Being a school dropout
- Being a "disconnected youth" (out of school and out of work)
- Being a teenage parent (or the child of a teenage parent)
- Being a frail elderly person

○ **Risk factors.** These are malleable conditions that point to a significant probability that the individuals, families, or groups who exhibit them will face major challenges to their present well-being and future prospects. Examples include:

- Chronic or acute illness
- Having a poor record of school attendance
- Being on course to fail in school or drop out
- Engaging in behaviors that can lead to teenage pregnancy
- Engaging in behaviors that can lead to incarceration
- Engaging in behaviors that can lead to social isolation
- Showing signs of clinical conditions that interfere with functioning
- Lacking adequate social or adaptive skills
- Lacking self-efficacy with regard to school, work, parenting, or participating in community affairs
- Engaging in behaviors that can lead to homelessness

Once an organization has codified its target population using both demographic and baseline indicators, it has to make its target population operational in a two-step process:

Step 1: ***Enrollment assessment*** consists of efforts to assess potential enrollees to ensure that they fit the profile of people whom the agency serves in order to meet its mission. This can be done either as part of a centralized enrollment process or as part of decentralized outreach efforts. What is essential is that all screeners use the same indicators and methods to assess them.

Step 2: ***Baseline assessment*** uses the risk-related indicators to identify crucial information about each client's situation and to specify the areas that the agency will address through its programming. But it may not elect to aim its services at ameliorating all such risk factors. Indeed, few agencies could do so. Rather, an organization will most often focus on a few risk indicators that it considers key, and about which it has the competencies and capacity to do something. The other risk factors it has identified will be used to develop a rich understanding of each client's situation so that services can be delivered more effectively.

> *The baseline assessment will generally be pulled together into a service plan that, among other things, specifies the short-term and intermediate outcomes that the organization has adopted and that staff (and/or volunteers) will be helping the client achieve.*

An agency might decide, for example, to enroll criminal gang members living in certain neighborhoods. But even though there are countless issues the organization could address in working with them, it might decide to focus only on unemployment as a risk indicator. Hence employment-related items such as work-readiness skills and work-related self-efficacy must be assessed at baseline after enrollment, and it will be for these indicators that the agency selects outcomes and engages in activities to promote them.

Rarely will an organization enroll only members of the target population in its programs. So it is also important for the organization to identify the wider range of people to whom it offers limited supports and opportunities such as access to computers and the Internet, information, free meeting space, or entertainment. As discussed earlier, the people in this larger group can be thought of as the agency's "service population," and the agency will not expect to produce outcomes for them. (The distinction between "target" and "service" populations will become critical in the discussion of "core" versus "supportive" programming discussed below under Day Three.)

Returning again to our extended example of the Children's Aid Society, the agency adopted the following four indicators to identify its target population:

Demographic profile

1. ***Socioeconomic status:*** children whose families are living in poverty
2. ***Age range:*** children starting at birth[32]
3. ***Geographical area:*** children must live or go to school in one of the neighborhoods CAS has targeted for its work

Risk profile

4. Beyond poverty, children exhibit ***key risk factors*** for poor life outcomes[33]

IN FOCUS

An Exercise in Thinking About Target and Service Populations

If you are a direct-service provider, fill in the blanks below for one of your core programs.

If you are a funder, fill in the blanks using what you know about a core program of one of your grantees.

32. The group referred for further study the question of the upper age limit, although this would certainly be in the high teens or low twenties.
33. The group referred for further study the selection of those risk factors on which CAS would focus.

If you are a consultant or a technical-assistance provider, fill in the blanks using what you know about a core program of one of your client organizations.

Name and kind of program (e.g., home services for the elderly, outreach services for homeless people, after-school programming for middle school children):

Target Population (individuals, families, or groups who are enrolled because the program is intended to improve their lives or prospects measurably):

- **Demographic Indicators:**

- **Risk Indicators:**

Service Population (people to whom the agency or program provides services without expecting to produce outcomes—perhaps, for example, in a drop-in center, through community-based informative workshops, or at a soup kitchen):

- **Demographic Indicators:**

- **Risk Indicators:**

Sometimes the meeting will flow more easily if the sequence moves directly from clarifying or reformulating the mission to discussing the target population that the organization exists to serve (or will elect to serve going forward). In any event, the foregoing discussion should make it plain how the process moves from the rather abstract statement of its mission downward through goals and objectives, finally reaching very concrete, operationally focused decisions about its target and service populations. Each level progressively constrains the options of the levels below it in a funneling process that leads to the creation of very clear parameters within which staff and management will be expected to work. At the end of this day, it is helpful to point out how the process has worked, where the challenges have been, and how these were addressed—and to thank participants for their hard work.

Summary of Day One

The facilitator guides the team of workshop participants through a sequence of discussions in which the group reaches binding decisions (or the executive director outlines a process for reaching those decisions that can't be settled during the day) in the following order:

- **Mission**—a succinct statement of the organization's value proposition that requires clarity and specificity about why the organization is doing its work, where it is doing its work, and how it is doing its work
- **Key strategic goals**—brief statements about what the organization must accomplish to succeed in its mission (usually over a five-year period); the fewer the better!
- **Objectives**—a list of the measurable milestones the organization will use to monitor progress toward the achievement of its goals
- **Target and service populations**—for the target populations, an unambiguous statement of the population the organization is committed to helping achieve specific outcomes through participation in its programming, with both demographic and risk indicators used in identifying the population; for service populations, a statement of the broadest aggregate of people who may access services that are meant to be supportive, but not to drive the achievement of outcomes

At the end of the day, the facilitator asks the note-taker to read these decisions and announces that the next day's work will start with an opportunity for the group to revisit any of them except the mission.

It is important to acknowledge the difficulty of this work and the specific challenges the group encountered and overcame.

Finally, it is helpful to remind participants that the work of the next day will be on client outcomes for target population members enrolled in core programs.

Day Two: Intended Outcomes

The second day should begin with a review of the prior day's work. Participants may well have been thinking about things overnight, and most likely they will need to revisit some decisions that were reached. Once these decisions are reaffirmed or amended, the work of the second day begins.

This is the day for the organization to select and codify the outcomes it will use to define the social value of its work measurably and meaningfully. Here it is useful to help the agency understand the difference between outputs and outcomes, and also between outcomes and impacts. As a reminder of what was said above:

> ***Outputs*** *consist of the number and kinds of people served, activities performed, and items produced by an organization during a given period (generally a year).*

One output that social service agencies tend to keep track of is the number of people they serve each year. Sometimes called a "turnstile" number, it tells us nothing about how service recipients benefited, what percentage achieved these benefits, or how many people received services at an intense enough level or participated long enough for them to benefit. Yet most government contracts and grant requirements settle for reports on turnstile counts as sufficient to indicate that a nonprofit organization is doing its work well, as long as the number is high enough. *Turnstile numbers are a pervasively used indicator for social impact in the nonprofit sector—an indicator that, in reality, tells us nothing at all about how or to what degree there has been any societal benefit produced!* As seductive as a gross turnstile count might be, it is not a meaningful measure to calculate the social good generated by a program (Hunter and Koopmans 2006).

The same can be said for any counting of outputs—whether they are in products produced (such as HIV- or smoking-prevention pamphlets printed) or activities undertaken (pamphlets distributed, meals served). By themselves these products and activities have little sustainable social value; no meaningful changes arise from their production and/or distribution alone. This poses a problem for funders and practitioners alike, because grants and contracts pay for the purchase of outputs (products and activities) and in fact cannot ever be used to purchase outcomes. No amount of money will ever buy healthier families, better-educated children, safer neighborhoods, fewer teenage parents, employment for the chronically unemployed, psychological stability for people with severe psychiatric disorders, or any other outcome.

> *Money buys outputs. Smart, intentional, and relentless management of outputs generates outcomes!*

So from the perspective of producing social impact and understanding the costs and benefits of doing so, linking revenues to outputs simply will not do the job. Even though it will inevitably be indirect, the funding of outputs must always must be linked to their use in achieving outcomes.

> **Outcomes.** *These are the expected, measurable changes undergone or achieved by service recipients participating in an agency's core programming—generally comprising changes in attitudes, knowledge, skills, behavior, status, and social or personal condition. These changes should be measured and monitored as part of an organization's work; they should link directly to the efforts of its staff (or volunteers) and serve as the basis for accountability.*[34] It is convenient to think about outcomes in terms of time, and to designate them as short-term (or immediate), intermediate, and long-term (or ultimate).

Long-term outcomes are those changes in service recipients that constitute the ultimate expression of the social value created

34. This definition of outcomes is framed from the point of view of performance management. Evaluators would not care whether they are measured and monitored by a given organization or program itself as part of its operations, nor whether they are used as the basis of an accountability system. Rather, the only questions evaluators would ask concern the degree to which these changes occur (the number and percentage of service recipients who manifest them) and to what extent they are attributable to a specific program or service.

by an organization. Usually they are assessed at some period after program participants are no longer receiving services. Hence long-term outcomes are not under an organization's direct control; rather, there is an expectation that they will be achieved, because the program has sufficiently prepared or equipped participants for achieving them (much as a vaccination equips people to resist disease). Long-term outcomes provide the definitive basis for examining what an organization does, how it does it, and with whom it does it. As the old saying goes, "If you don't know where you are going, all roads will get you there!"

Long-Term Outcomes Used by Youth Villages

Youth Villages—headquartered in Memphis, TN, and currently serving high-risk[35] children and teens and their families in a dozen states (counting the District of Columbia) through residential and community-based services—tracks long-term outcomes for its program participants six, twelve, and twenty-four months after discharge. At twenty-four months after discharge, 85 percent of service recipients are in high school, have graduated from high school, or are in GED classes; of those in school, 88 percent have mostly passing grades, 88 percent have not been suspended or expelled, and 91 percent are not truant; 82 percent have not been in trouble with the law; and 81 percent are living at home with family or independently, while only 18 percent of youth under age eighteen are in state custody[36] (Youth Villages 2011).

And with regard to our extended example, the Children's Aid Society has decided that it will measure its long-term outcomes using one of two indicators as appropriate to the individual young person: at age twenty-six the service recipient will have graduated from, or will be enrolled in and on track to complete, post-secondary education, or he or she will be employed full-time and living above poverty.

35. These risk factors include mental illness, domestic violence, substance abuse, criminal behavior and other legal issues, and having experienced abuse.

36. These outcomes are only for program participants who received at least sixty days of service.

Since long-term outcomes are measured some period of time after the organization has discharged its clients, the outcomes can be achieved only indirectly. Program participants must reach a level of preparation, adaptation, and resilience by the time they leave the program that makes it very likely that they can and will achieve the long-term outcomes as intended. This level of client readiness to achieve long-term outcomes constitutes what is often the end of a series of outcomes. Returning to the example of the psychiatric hospital I led, adopting a score of 65 on the Global Assessment of Functioning scale as the single intermediate outcome was of central importance in helping us treat our patients better and discharge them sooner.

Intermediate outcomes are the changes in service recipients that one expects to see at specific points or intervals while they are participating in a program. Intermediate outcomes are convenient milestones for knowing that participants are benefiting as intended from services and making progress (in what the agency has specified as a timely manner) toward readiness for discharge from the program. Achievement of such outcomes strongly predicts the likelihood that the discharged participants will go on to achieve the organization's targeted long-term outcomes.

IN FOCUS

Intermediate Outcomes Used by CAS

Here are the intermediate outcomes that CAS will focus on for the adolescents and young adults it serves in its core programming:[37]

- The child/youth is fluent in English.
- The youth gets into what CAS regards as a "good" high school.
- The high school student passes the Regents Examinations.
- The high school student passes Advanced Placement courses.
- The high school student achieves good enough PSAT/SAT scores to qualify for college matriculation.

37. Note the educational focus. This is because CAS understands that, in the United States, high educational attainment is the most reliable ladder that children of low-income parents can use to escape from poverty.

- The high school student graduates with a HS diploma.
- The high school dropout earns a GED.
- The young adult enters post-secondary education (final intermediate outcome).

These intermediate outcomes constitute a logical sequence of necessary milestones to track the progress of teens toward the ultimate outcomes that CAS has targeted.

Finally, we arrive at short-term outcomes.

Short-term outcomes are immediate, incremental changes that service recipients achieve in direct and easily understood relation to the services they receive or program activities in which they participate. High-performing service providers track such data weekly or even daily in order to be sure they are optimizing their influence on the intended beneficiaries, and making immediate ("real time") adjustments in what they are doing, how they are doing it, or how much they are doing if clients are not making progress at targeted rates (a key performance standard).

IN FOCUS

Short-Term Outcomes Used by WINGS for kids

WINGS for kids, an after-school program headquartered in Charleston, SC, works with elementary school children from low-income families to help them develop social and emotional skills (widely regarded as essential building blocks for subsequent academic and social success). WINGS has codified a sequence of very short-term outcomes that it measures daily and tracks weekly for every participant:

Outcome 1. The kids[38] know about SEL[39]

- Kids can recite 1 element of the WINGS creed[40]
- Kids can recite 2 elements of the WINGS creed

38. This is the term WINGS for kids uses to designate program participants.

39. "SEL" stands for "Social and Emotional Learning."

40. The WINGS creed is a series of statements developed by participating kids and professional staff; these statements articulate the importance of self-respect, mutual respect, constructive conflict resolution, academic and related kinds of self-efficacy, and setting high goals. Kids and staff recite it daily. The ability to recite the WINGS creed shows that participants have learned specific ideas about healthy ways to be and act in the world. Outcome 2 shows the ability to apply the knowledge conceptually; and Outcome 3 shows changes in behavior that express the values and ideas of the creed.

- Kids can recite 3 elements of the WINGS creed
- Kids can recite 4 elements of the WINGS creed
- Kids can recite 5 elements of the WINGS creed

Outcome 2. The kids understand SEL

- Kids can give a meaningful example of 1 creed element from their lives
- Kids can give a meaningful example of 2 creed elements from their lives
- Kids can give a meaningful example of 3 creed elements from their lives
- Kids can give a meaningful example of 4 creed elements from their lives
- Kids can give a meaningful example of 5 creed elements from their lives

Outcome 3. The kids pass frequent tests demonstrating their mastery of:

- Self-awareness
- Social awareness
- Responsible decision making
- Relationship skills
- Self-management

Consider the Center for Employment Opportunities (CEO), which works with prisoners leaving incarceration in three states (seven jurisdictions) by placing them on transitional work crews in order to help them become job-ready and avoid recidivism. This is how the agency discusses "tracking participant outcomes" on its website:

> *Once participants have begun transitional employment on CEO work crews, their daily attendance* [i.e., a program performance standard] *as well as their progress in developing appropriate on-the-job behaviors and basic skills* [i.e., short-term outcomes] *is noted daily in their Passport to Success booklets. Collected Passport data is then entered into the Salesforce.com database and analyzed*

> *to determine when participants have achieved baseline preparation for full-time employment* [i.e., intermediate outcome] *in the competitive workforce. Once this milestone is achieved, participants are considered "job start ready" and begin interviewing for full-time positions identified by Job Developers in CEO's vocational services teams.*[41]

CEO's long-term outcomes and impacts are shown below.

Long-Term Outcomes and Impacts Used by CEO

In 2004, CEO, the Center for Employment Opportunities, was selected to be part of a national, multi-site study of programs serving populations that are "hard to employ," which certainly describes the prisoners reentering society whom CEO serves. The research was conducted by MDRC, a highly regarded evaluation organization. CEO was required, as part of this evaluation, to participate in a randomized control trial (RCT) in which potential program participants were selected randomly from eligible individuals (New York State prisoners being released) and then compared with those who had not been selected—a method that eliminates most non-program factors as explanations for why outcomes are achieved.

Two years after discharge from the program, CEO's graduates (the intervention group) showed a significant reduction in criminal convictions and incarceration for a new crime—better (at a statistically significant level of confidence) than the outcomes for the control group, the study participants who were not part of the CEO program. These long-term outcomes are thus legitimately recognized as the impact of CEO's programming—and indeed are very important and unusual. (By the way, these impacts were notably stronger for reentering prisoners who were engaged quickly upon their release, rather than three months later.) It is worth noting that even though CEO focuses on and monitors employment readiness and fully expected employment to be a long-term impact, the MDRC study showed that unsubsidized employment is in fact less of a robust long-term program impact of CEO programming than the reduction in criminal convictions (Redcross, Millensky, and Rudd 2012). Hence policy analysts should consider whether even brief or subsidized employment—not in themselves

41. My own clarifying notes are added in brackets.

very significant outcomes—might nonetheless have a powerful impact on long-term criminal recidivism, especially if reentering prisoners are engaged in work-related programming very quickly upon their release.

Impacts are outcomes that can, using experimental research methods, be attributed (with a great deal of confidence)[42] to the effects on participants of a program or service.[43] Whereas measuring outcomes requires only the tracking of program participants, understanding impact requires that the outcomes achieved by service recipients and the percentage of program participants who have achieved them be compared with those of similar—or, if possible, identical—groups who have not received these services. Making a comparison with a control group is the only way one can eliminate alternative explanations—for instance, that sometimes people make progress on their own—for why individuals or groups achieved the changes that are being tracked. Going back to a previous example, until WINGS for kids compares how much SEL its program participants have mastered with how much SEL similar children exhibit who are not in its programs, it is impossible to know whether the SEL outcomes that the organization tracks for participating kids are due to the programs or whether they have simply come about as a result of normal family, neighborhood, and school experiences.[44]

Or consider the fact that a majority of the job placements (impacts) claimed by some famous government programs to help unemployed individuals get and keep employment were shown, by evaluations, to be due to general, normal job-seeking behavior and therefore were not in any way affected by program participation (Gueron 2005).[45]

42. Generally, with a degree of confidence of 95 percent.

43. This is the definition of impacts that most evaluators would use. However, it is worth noting that in popular usage the term often is used to mean something else entirely—namely, the long-term consequences attributable to some degree (if even loosely) to a program or service or other kind of intervention (see, e.g., Penna 2011: 19-20). In the framework of this chapter, that definition would apply to the concept of "long-term outcome" or "ultimate outcome"—but not to "impact."

44. Aware of this issue, WINGS for kids is currently planning a series of external evaluations that will ultimately show whether its SEL outcomes are due to its program.

45. The U.S. Job Training Partnership Act and the New York State Employment and Training Choices programs. (Yes, the results of the evaluations mean that it is fair to suggest that these programs were a waste of money . . . lots of money!)

Once the long-term outcomes are specified in measurable terms, and the period for which they will be tracked has been established, then the conversation can flow logically to the conditions that service recipients will have to achieve in order to make it very likely that they will attain the long-term outcomes. As noted above, these conditions constitute the last of a sequence of intermediate outcomes. And as with the long-term outcomes themselves, the indicators and measures that will be used to monitor them (and the intervals at which they will be measured) must be specified.

Finally, once it is clear what intermediate outcomes must be achieved, it will be relatively easy to establish the short-term outcome "staircases" of incremental change that will carry service recipients to intermediate outcomes (like those shown in the examples above). If the sequence is reversed—that is, if short-term outcomes are selected before intermediate outcomes—it will be almost impossible to help the group fight its way out of the thicket of the myriad possible short-term outcomes it might track.

Tips for Selecting, Codifying, and Measuring Outcomes

Measuring outcomes is a lot less difficult than most people think. The hard part is settling on the optimal outcome sequence for members of a (well-delineated and deeply understood) target population. Once this conceptual work is done—and it is essential for any agency claiming to help people improve their lives or prospects to do that work—then the means to measure short-term and intermediate outcomes become quite obvious. There are really only three ways to measure outcomes:

Yes/no assessments. These involve determining whether something has happened or not. Generally this is pretty easy: A student graduates from high school with a diploma or doesn't. A woman is pregnant or isn't. A released prisoner re-offends or doesn't, is re-incarcerated or isn't. A patient dies or doesn't, a citizen votes or doesn't, a job seeker gets employment (however defined) or doesn't.

Outcomes measured in a yes/no way have the virtue of being very clear and easy to understand. They are useful for understanding how individuals have benefited from a program, and also for calculating aggregated program effectiveness. Yes/no assessments are thus helpful in measuring long-term and even intermediate progress, both of which take significant time to manifest themselves. Their "all or nothing" quality makes them quite useless, however, for tracking program participants' incremental progress (or noting their lack of progress) toward short-term outcomes. That progress must be monitored so that staff and managers of social service programs can make adjustments quickly if clients are not benefiting as expected.

Clients' incremental progress toward short-term outcomes can best be measured in the following ways:

- **Numerical assessments.** These involve counting things. How many days per week does a child attend school? How many days per week does a frail elderly person leave his or her home? Out of a required repertoire of hard (vocation-based) skills, how many has a prospective employee mastered? On a depression checklist, how many items does a patient exhibit?

  Numerical assessments also have the virtue of clarity, and their quantifiable nature makes them easy to use for tracking progress by individual clients and also for understanding clients' aggregated progress toward short-term outcomes for the entire program. (And similarly they are useful for measuring intermediate and long-term outcomes.)

  However, not all socially meaningful short-term outcomes are things that can be measured meaningfully by counting. Fortunately, there is another way to measure incremental progress on short-term outcomes—one that allows the monitoring of what are usually considered qualitative effects and therefore often lie close to the hearts of social service practitioners. These are:

- **Scale-based assessments.** Outcome scales consist of "ladders" or "staircases" with measurable steps that program participants can move up on their way to achieving intermediate outcomes. Does a youth have antisocial attitudes? Does a first grader have academic self-efficacy? How well is a psychiatric patient functioning? How constructively does an employee participate as a team member? How optimistic is a frail elderly person that life can offer worthwhile rewards?

  All such questions can be answered using scales that start at the lowest level and move incrementally toward a desirable level. Some scales are based on statements that the client responds to along a continuum from "strong disagreement" to "strong agreement."

> Others, such as the Global Assessment of Functioning scale that I used when I managed the psychiatric hospital, have a standardized set of steps with a definition for each step, against which program participants can be matched to the level that most accurately captures their condition or how they are doing. But for this kind of scale, only one variable can change from one step to the next. If two or more variables change, then assigning a new level on the scale to a client could mean either that he or she has made progress in relation to one variable but not the other, or that he or she has made progress in relation to both variables—and it is impossible to know which is the case without access to accompanying notes. (All too frequently one sees agencies using scales in which more than one variable changes from one level to the next—evaluators call them "double-barreled scales." In theory-of-change workshops, double-barreled outcome scales must be identified and fixed.)
>
> When scales are designed well, they can be used to assess almost any qualitative matter, and therefore put to rest fears that performance measurement necessarily reduces social services to simplistic, reductionist, or almost meaningless measurements. It is best if an organization uses scales that have been tested and validated for the populations they serve. But sometimes this isn't practical, either because such scales have not been produced with regard to the phenomenon that is the focus of the agency's work, or because the scale is too complex or costly to use (in time, effort, or money to pay for copyrighted materials). In such cases it is perfectly legitimate for the organization to develop its own scales (or pay someone to do so) and to use them to measure and monitor client progress. Doing so systematically will reveal whether they need to be modified—if, for instance, clients who do not end up achieving the agency's intermediate outcomes have shown misleading incremental progress on the scales. At some point, of course, such "homegrown" scales should have their validity assessed by a formative evaluation, as discussed above.
>
> The neat thing about scales, though, is that they allow one to treat very nuanced, complex, and qualitative matters quantitatively by assigning a numeric value to each step on a scale. This allows for aggregated data analysis, which is essential for driving organizational learning and quality improvement.

Some of this thinking is inspired by the seminal work of Alvan R. Feinstein (1977). Practitioners looking for a wealth of information about outcome indicators and measures to use should visit www.Childtrends.org and www.PerformWell.org, to name but a few examples.

While it is essential for the workshop group as a whole to identify the organization's long-term outcomes, it is not feasible for the large group to work on intermediate and short-term outcomes. Therefore, once the long-term outcomes have been established, generally it is a good idea to use breakout sessions for the members of individual programs, or other groupings of participants that the leader identifies, to codify the intermediate and short-term outcomes that they find meaningful, then report to the group as a whole for discussion and final decisions about which outcomes to adopt and what indicators to use.[46] The selection of specific measures (including the design of scales) should be left for later—that is, as part of the organization's work to implement the decisions reached in the workshop.

Summary of Day Two

After giving the group a chance to review its work on Day One and raise any concerns or address requests for reconsideration of any items (except the mission statement), the facilitator leads the workshop participants through a discussion of the outcomes the organization will utilize to manage and evaluate its performance.

- First, outcomes are defined as the expected, measurable changes undergone or achieved by service recipients participating in an agency's core programming—generally comprising changes in attitudes, knowledge, skills, behavior, status, and social or personal condition. These changes should be monitored as part of an organization's work, link directly to the efforts of its staff (or volunteers), and serve as the basis for accountability.
- Next, the facilitator explains the nature of long-term, intermediate, and short-term outcomes, and notes that performance management focuses on the third one while evaluation focuses on the other two. (See Appendix I, which discusses the differences between performance management and evaluation.)

46. It is best if the same short-term outcome measures are used across all or most programs in an agency.

- If the organization has more than one outcome-producing program, the facilitator asks the group to consider the overarching or agency-wide long-term and intermediate outcomes for which the organization holds itself accountable as the measurable expression of its value proposition.
- For each long-term and intermediate outcome, the group should select the indicators it will measure to assess whether the outcome has been achieved. This amounts to producing an operational definition of each outcome.
- Next, it is useful to have breakout groups, and ask each of them to develop a list of the short-term outcomes their program produces that drive to one or more of the intermediate outcomes identified at the corporate level. In essence, program-level final outcomes must be identical to the indicators for overarching or agency-wide outcomes.
- Bringing the group back into plenary session, the facilitator requests reports from the breakout sessions. The entire group then considers the outcomes claimed by each program, "stress-tests" them for credibility in relation to what the program actually does, identifies gaps in short-term outcomes that the group deems essential to help enrolled target population members achieve the corporate outcomes, decides whether these gaps are "mission-critical," and considers the programmatic implications of these discussions. This final topic will become the focus of Day Three.

Day Three: Programs and Services

On Days One and Two the organization established the conditions for designing its programs and services: first by clarifying whom they are meant to help (the target population) and then by establishing the progression of outcomes that service recipients should achieve through a sequence of short-term and intermediate outcomes on the way to ultimate (long-term) outcomes.[47]

Day Three is devoted to the codification of programs and services.

Step 1: Review of Current Program Models/Designs

Here it is helpful to introduce the distinction between core programming (the "egg yolk" in Figure 1, below), which is intended to produce outcomes for target population participants, and supportive programming (the "egg white"), which is meant to be engaging and even helpful but without the expectation that it will produce outcomes.

Supportive programming typically consists of such things as recreational activities, creative/expressive opportunities, one-session workshops, outreach, drop-in and resource centers, soup kitchens, and shelters. Although these programs (or program elements) are not designed to produce outcomes, their outputs can be of great value and meet significant needs. The challenge of managing such services is to maintain high quality: meals served should be nutritious, shelter beds should be clean and the environment safe, creative/expressive activities should be led by highly qualified staff or volunteers, and workshops should be meaningful and well taught.

Core programming requires managing effectiveness in addition to managing quality. This is the subject of Day Four: performance management. On this day, current program elements and services should be reviewed for evidence that they are likely to be effective in moving the specified target population members through the outcome sequences developed during Day Three. Often this will involve referring to repositories of evidence-based program information—either by research or through engaging participants' expert knowledge.

47. It is essential that the workshop follow this sequence, even though it is counterintuitive for many social service practitioners who are used to focusing on what they do—their programmatic activities and services—but not to thinking deeply about why or to what effect they are engaging in their work. Unless the facilitator is alert to this tendency and takes an active role in directing the conversation, discussions of outcomes will quickly morph into discussions of "what we do."

Figure 1. Core Programming and Supportive Programming

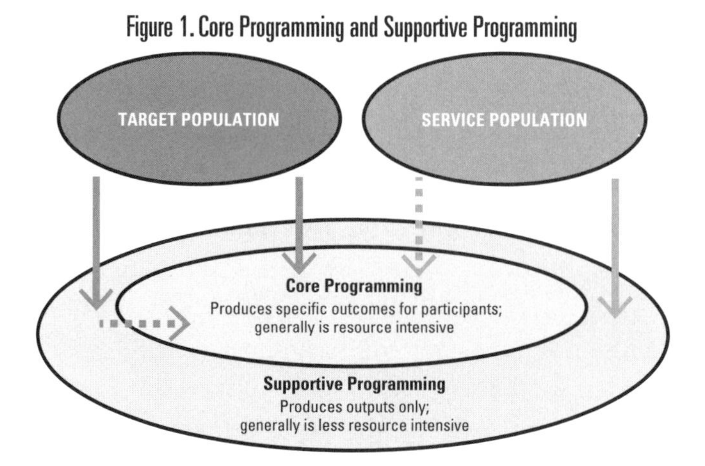

Step 2: Selection of Program and Service Elements

The staff should be urged to decide whether to keep programming as is, make specific adjustments, add new services to improve the overall effectiveness of their work, and/or eliminate aspects of their work that they have come to see as ineffective or as a distraction from the agency's mission. In this context, it is important for the facilitator to know at least as much as (or, preferably, more than) the workshop participants about evidence-based practices in the domains under consideration. In this way the facilitator has sufficient gravitas to drive what will often be very challenging discussions in which providers will be asked to give up pet practices and habitual methods in order to serve people better.

Step 3: Program and Service Codification

Once the array of program elements and services has been selected as the basis for the agency's work (going forward) with its target population, these must be codified. This means establishing *implementation standards*, which essentially answer the questions of what, who, where, how much, how often, how long, and how well:

What—the menu of activities that staff (and/or volunteers) will provide (e.g., mentoring, tutoring, case management, experiential learning, supported employment)

Who—the competencies needed to provide these activities (e.g., language and cultural competencies, ability to conduct motivational interviews)

Where—the location and modality through which the activities will be provided (e.g., home-based, center-based, in-person group or individual, via telephone)

How much—the dosage per occasion that a service recipient should receive (generally measured in time)

How often—the frequency with which service recipients should participate in each activity (e.g., daily, several times per week, weekly)

How long—the time period for which program participation should last in order for clients to benefit as intended (e.g., a couple of hours, as with a one-time workshop; three to four months, as with Multisystemic Therapy; two and a quarter years, as with the Nurse-Family Partnership)

How well—the indicators that the organization will track to be sure that services are of a high level of quality (e.g., high participation rates, participant satisfaction)

In addition, for each core program or service it is essential to list the outcomes that it is intended to produce.

Table 3, for example, shows how HarborCOV, an agency that works with domestic violence victims and survivors in the Greater Boston area, made sure that all of its programs contributed to the overarching outcomes—that is, the agency-wide outcomes, those for which the agency holds itself accountable—for the people to whom it is committed.[48] On Day Two, the agency identified the overarching, long-term outcomes shown in Table 3.[49]

48. This information is presented with the permission of Lynn Peters and Kourou Pich, HarborCOV's co-directors.

49. This was an enormous step forward. The agency had never identified such outcomes before, and indeed had trouble identifying outcomes even at the program level. Certainly it had never before held any staff members responsible for managing to outcomes. In fact, its "trauma-informed" approach to service delivery had made it very difficult for the staff to even think about outcomes at any level other than those goals personally selected by each survivor. The immensity of the cultural shift required of staff members to implement a results-driven approach to performance management was marked by their deciding to change the designation of front-line staff from "advocates" to "case managers," with the associated responsibility of promoting and tracking outcomes specified by the agency, not just those selected by the people served.

Table 3. HarborCOV's Long-Term Outcomes,[50] Indicators, and Measures[51]

LONG-TERM OUTCOMES	INDICATORS	MEASURES
1. Living violence-free	No instances of domestic abuse for at least a year	Client self-reports collected every six months after discharge
2. Have stable housing	Housing is safe, and individual (or family) is under no immediate pressure to leave	Client self-reports collected every six months after discharge
3. Have a sustainable income[52]	To be developed[53]	Client self-reports collected every six months after discharge
4. Have completed two years of post-secondary education[54]	Credits or degrees earned	Review of transcripts or certificates
5. Legal U.S. resident status achieved (for undocumented individuals only)	U.S. federal documentation	Review of federal documentation

After clarifying its long-term outcomes, HarborCOV identified the core programs that it would hold accountable for contributing to its ability to deliver these outcomes to all intended beneficiaries. In essence, this meant that the specific program outcomes should be the

50. These outcomes are for clients who left the program at least a year earlier.

51. "Indicators" are the categories of data that are assessed to identify whether an outcome has been achieved; "measures" are the means used to make these assessments.

52. HarborCOV will create a formula for assessing this based on federal guidelines for the Greater Boston area.

53. It is often not possible for all codification decisions to be made within the context of a theory-of-change workshop. However, it is essential to identify and document each such decision to be made, and for the agency's leaders to design processes for making the decisions soon after the workshop has ended.

54. Possibilities include two years of a four-year college, a completed associate's degree, or completion of a professional certification program.

indicators that HarborCOV would use to measure its corporate outcomes. The three core programs it identified were Case Management, Housing, and Specialized Services.

Here we shall look only at the agency's codification of its Case Management program.

The HarborCOV Case Management Program

Case Management is the point of entry into all HarborCOV core programs.[55]

Overseen by the director of programs and services, the program is staffed by case managers and provides the following services:

- Hotline emergency response
- Initial (telephone-based) pre-assessment[56]
- External referrals for individuals who are not part of the target population
- Internal referral for Initial Intake Assessment (enrollment) and the High-Risk and Intimate Partner Screening Tools for members of the target population
- Initial Intake Assessment to assure appropriateness of enrollment
- A General (second) Assessment process for enrolled clients[57]
- Development of an Individualized Service Plan (ISP) and an Individualized Goal Plan (IGP)[58]
- Internal referrals for HarborCOV's Housing Program and Specialized Services as indicated

55. To be clear: no clients can be entered into any core programming without first being enrolled in Case Management. The sequence of client assessments described below will be built into the HarborCOV performance-management data system. Some of the assessment items will come directly from assessments that are required by contracts or state law, regulations, or procedures.

56. This will result in the identification of people who do not meet HarborCOV's definition of its target population and who should be referred externally or to peripheral HarborCOV programming such as Domestic Violence Education groups, and also the identification of target population members who should be admitted to Case Management for a deeper assessment. This is the first of a sequence of three progressively more comprehensive assessments that Case Management provides—leading to a baseline for service planning and the tracking of subsequent client progress toward achieving targeted outcomes.

57. Baseline assessment should include all short-term and intermediate outcome assessment items used in the three core programs.

58. While some goals on these plans may be unique to individual clients, the core of the ISPs and IGPs should focus on HarborCOV's program-based short-term outcomes and rely on the use of a standardized list of services and referrals.

- External referrals to vetted[59] service provides as indicated
- Weekly client contact, including at least two one-hour face-to-face solution-focused meetings per month, that help clients achieve targeted outcomes by reviewing their ISP and IGP
- Tracking of incremental client progress toward outcomes
- Periodic case reviews to optimize services so clients will benefit as quickly and completely as possible
- Forward-looking exit planning, with encouragement of the client to focus on the five HarborCOV long-term outcomes: (a) living violence-free, (b) acquiring stable housing, (c) gaining a sustainable income, (d) completing two years of post-secondary education, and (e) gaining legal U.S. resident status (for undocumented individuals only)

These services are provided by case managers with caseloads of twenty clients each—eight clients in HarborCOV housing and twelve who are community-based.

Case Management staff must meet the following background expectations and competencies:

Director of Programs and Services

Background Expectations

- No less than five years of highly relevant experience required, and/or master's degree in social work, public health, or related field; licensure preferred
- Computer literacy
- Bilingual (Spanish)/bicultural preferred

59. HarborCOV will need to undertake due diligence to determine the quality and effectiveness of the service providers to which it refers its Case Management clients.

Competency Requirements

- Clear understanding of the multiple issues that intersect in the lives of survivors
- Good written and oral communication skills
- Strong problem-solving skills
- Exceptional assessment, decision-making, and supervisory skills
- Ability to assess and deal constructively with emergencies or crises (especially where violence is involved)
- Ability to provide supportive supervision to front-line staff with regard to all service modalities, with a focus on results-based accountability
- Ability to use the HarborCOV performance-management data system in conformity with all policies and procedures (e.g., daily data entry, review of client progress to prepare for meetings)
- Ability to take initiative, desire to be held accountable
- Ability to work as part of a team
- Ability to work with discipline and demonstrate a high degree of professionalism

Case Manager[60]

Background Expectations

- No less than three years of highly relevant experience required
- Computer literacy
- Bilingual (Spanish)/bicultural preferred

60. HarborCOV plans to add a case manager position, bringing the total to four.

Competency Requirements

- Strong listening, communication, and solution-focused problem-solving skills
- Ability to communicate fluently in English and/or Spanish
- Knowledge of community-based resources, especially in low-income communities
- Ability to assess and deal constructively with emergencies or crises (especially where violence is involved)
- Ability to develop ISPs and IGPs using assessment data
- Ability to do a depression and suicide assessment
- Ability to make appropriate referrals (internal and external)
- Knowledge of solutions-focused interviewing, and ability to provide solutions-focused services
- Ability to run groups—with mastery of group processes and contents
- Ability to use the HarborCOV performance-management data system in conformity with all policies and procedures (e.g., daily data entry, review of client progress to prepare for meetings)
- Ability to staff the crisis hotline and make appropriate referrals
- Strong critical-thinking skills
- Ability to take initiative, desire to be held accountable
- Ability to work both independently and as part of a team
- Demonstrated understanding of culturally appropriate, strength-based strategies within an anti-racism, and economic and social justice, framework

In their day-to-day work, case managers focus on helping clients achieve the short-term and intermediate outcomes shown in Table 4.

Table 4. HarborCOV Case Management Program Outcomes, Indicators, and Measures

SHORT-TERM OUTCOMES	INDICATORS	MEASURES
1. Violence-free living	No incident of domestic violence since last report	Weekly client self-reports
2. Academic self-efficacy	Score on an academics-related self-efficacy scale	Scale (to be developed) administered no less than monthly
3. Work-related self-efficacy	Score on a work-related self-efficacy scale	Scale (to be developed) administered no less than monthly
4. Conversational English literacy	Ability to communicate effectively in English	Assessment to be developed
INTERMEDIATE OUTCOMES	**INDICATORS**	**MEASURES**
1–4. Same as short-term outcomes	Status of each outcome is sufficiently good that participants can be discharged from the program	Same

In order to ensure that clients receive the best services possible, HarborCOV will use the indicators shown in Table 5 to track the quality of the Case Management program.

Table 5. HarborCOV Case Management Program Quality Indicators

INDICATOR	MEASURES
1. Appropriate use of referrals	Referrals and their use by clients tracked as indicated in relationship to ISP and IGP by the case manager
2. Client utilization levels	Client participation in all scheduled activities tracked weekly by the case manager
3. Robust ISPs and IGPs with a focus on achieving a strong social support group in addition to the targeted intermediate outcomes	Monthly review of IGPs by the director of programs and services and the director of clinical services against a quality checklist (to be developed)
4. Client–case manager relationship	Weekly assessment of the case manager (scale to be developed) in terms of the degree to which the client is relying on the relationship to help solve problems, make plans, and take action

As the example of HarborCOV illustrates, Day Three requires going into detail. Again, breakout groups are essential—generally organized in terms of the professional groupings of staff, with managers attached to the groups for which they are responsible. It tends to be an exhausting day but sets the foundation for Day Four, where the topic is performance management.

Summary of Day Three

The facilitator asks the group to review the day's work and raise for discussion any items that are of concern, are unclear, or appear to require deeper exploration. Once this task has been completed, the facilitator guides the group through the following discussion sequence.

Step 1: Review of current program models/designs.

Step 2: Selection of program and service elements.

Step 3: Program and service codification. This consists of answering the following questions for each program or service:

1. **What**—the menu of activities that the staff (and/or volunteers) will provide
2. **Who**—the competencies needed to provide these activities
3. **Where**—the location and modality through which the activities will be provided
4. **How much**—the dosage that a service recipient should receive on each occasion
5. **How often**—the frequency with which service recipients should participate in each activity
6. **How long**—the period during which program participation should last in order for clients to benefit as intended
7. **How well**—the indicators that the organization will track in order to be sure that services are of a high level of quality

Day Four: Performance Management

The pillars and elements of performance management were discussed in Chapter 3. All the elements, tailored to each organization's current capacities, should be addressed on Day Four of the workshop. Typically, the areas that require the most focus and discussion are:

1. Leading and Managing

There is an anti-authoritarian sentiment that is widespread in the nonprofit sector. Relatedly, the Kantian imperative to treat people with respect has been conflated with the idea that everyone's opinions should carry equal weight. I have watched many an executive director struggle with the notion that she or he should set performance standards and hold people accountable for achieving them, and I have observed managers agonize over the need to give specific directions to front-line staff. But being an effective facilitator of this work requires that when such a hyper-egalitarian bias is encountered, it must be challenged. No organization can be relied on to deliver the goods when its leaders and managers won't take on the burdens of leading and managing. As I said in Chapter 3, leaders have to set and maintain an organization's strategic direction, and managers have to direct and support front-line staff in performing their work in ways that realize the organization's goals.

To me, this is a deal-killing area. If I cannot help an organization past these conflicts, I will have failed in my obligation to help it develop a blueprint for managing to outcomes and ultimately for achieving success. On rare occasions, upon reaching such a point of paralysis at a workshop, I have suggested that an organization stop the process and that we all pack our bags and go home. Also, on such occasions I suggested that I should not be paid. This has proved to be an extremely powerful intervention, and in the end, with only one exception (so far), all of my clients have found a way to internalize the need to lead and to manage.

2. Accountability

In a related vein, the concept of accountability tends to be alien to nonprofit organizations; it is often seen as an unwelcome, dehumanizing import from the corporate sector. But as Chapter 3 made clear, performance will be unreliable—fluctuating between good and bad, effective and ineffective—in the absence of a system of accountability. The comments I made with regard to the need to challenge organizational conflict having to do with leading and managing apply equally to the need to challenge ambivalence regarding the need to hold managers and staff members accountable. A facilitator who fails to do so is, in the end, legitimizing an obstacle to high performance.

3. Results-Focused Budgeting

Anyone familiar with the social sector recognizes that nonprofits operate in a funding environment that is capricious, fragmented, and categorical. Funders often refuse to support overhead costs adequately, thereby making it almost impossible for organizations to build the capacities and competencies to manage to outcomes. Add to this the fact that funders like to see their revenues spent in dedicated programs and services where expenditures can be tied very directly to specified activities, which undercuts one of money's most powerful characteristics: it is fungible (that is, it can be spent on whatever is needed). In *Billions of Drops in Millions of Buckets*, Steven Goldberg (2009) documents how these constraints reduce executive directors to the status of eternal panhandlers, preoccupying and exhausting them, and keeping them from focusing on how well their organization is performing.

In the course of the four-day workshop, discussions are often derailed by comments like:

> "Our funders don't pay us to do that."
>
> "Our funders won't pay more than 8 percent for overhead."

> "We can't focus on a target population because our funders want us to serve everybody."
>
> "We have more than enough money to run Program A well, but we can't shift any of it to build up Program B because these are categorical revenues."
>
> "We can't lower caseloads because our funders insist that we keep our unit-of-service costs low."
>
> "We can't spend our funders' money to improve program effectiveness because they want us to spend it on replicating."

The examples are endless, and endlessly destructive. There is truth to the complaints, but the workshop facilitator cannot buy in to the helplessness that the organization's leaders and staff members are expressing. Rather, I think it is essential to challenge the organization to manage differently.

First, it is worth observing that an organization that outsources its strategic and tactical management decisions to funders will ultimately undercut any claims that it deserves to be funded. An organization has to develop a clear value proposition and then find funders who will invest in it. That is the thrust of Day One of these workshops.

Second, it is essential to challenge the organization's board with regard to its fiduciary responsibilities. In these workshops I often comment along these lines: "As a board, you should recognize that every time your executive director lands another big grant or contract paying 10 percent overhead or less, it's actually weakening your organization. Why? Because the overhead required for managing a high-performing organization well will probably never be less than 25 percent. So rather than congratulating the executive director for another big 'get,' you should take a collective deep breath and figure out how you are going to raise the missing 15 percent of the grant's face value."

Third, the chief financial officer, together with the executive director, must be made aware that other organizations are in similar straits but have learned how to make their revenues more fungible, shifting them as needed across program boundaries to build capacity for managing to outcomes wherever necessary. Often it is very helpful to facilitate their contact with other organizations that have come up with creative ways to do this, and further, to make them aware of practical technical assistance services such as those provided by the Nonprofit Finance Fund.

Finally, it is worth pointing out that unless and until an organization has robust performance data, it has virtually no leg to stand on when approaching a funder to renegotiate terms of grants or contracts. Specifically, it is essential to know, in aggregated numbers, (a) who is getting services, (b) exactly what the services comprise, (c) what the evidentiary basis is for the design of these services, (d) how clients are utilizing services, (e) how well clients are succeeding in achieving targeted outcomes, and (f) what infrastructure and other overhead costs are associated with effective service delivery. When funders are pressing for the expansion or replication of services, it is critical that an organization understand that adequate funding will not only require a commensurate multiple of the service delivery costs per added unit of service, but also will require up-front growth capital to pay for expanded infrastructure, extended management capacity, and various startup costs in new locations.

An organization that does not have an adequate performance-management data system will be unable to meet these challenges. Most likely it will forever limp along—working extremely hard but not very well.

That is why, on the final day of the workshop, the last key task is:

4. Performance Measurement and Monitoring

A high-performing organization needs a single performance-management data system for the organization as a whole—and for each program, service, and/or local site. This entails clearly articulating what data to track, how to interpret and use these data, and how staff will be held accountable for managing to outcomes and for maintaining high quality (or just the latter in the case of supportive—rather than core—programs like drop-in centers).

Generally, the tasks that need to be covered on this day are:

- **Specifying the criteria that the organization will use to select or improve its performance-management data system.** At a minimum, such a system should:
  - Be web-based
  - Allow for distributed data entry and retrieval for all front-line staff
  - Permit the tracking of client enrollment data (demographic and baseline)
  - Monitor program-utilization data (dosages received, frequency of attendance, duration of participation)
  - Be able to identify characteristics of those who don't participate at the expected levels or who fail to complete the program as intended
  - Track incremental achievement of short-term outcomes by all core program participants in "real time"
  - Document the attainment of intermediate and long-term outcomes
  - Monitor service quality indicators
  - Allow for easy ways in which to analyze and learn about correlations among staff efforts, program utilization by service recipients, the achievement of outcomes by service recipients, and the impact on program participation and the achievement of outcomes by variations in level of program or service quality
- **Clarifying the data sets that supervisors will review with front-line staff to help them improve the effectiveness of their work.** At a minimum, staff members should be required to enter information about clients' utilization of services and progress in achieving short-term and intermediate outcomes. Both supervisors and staff should know exactly

what the metrics are, how they are expected to shift over time, and how to use patterns to identify where things are going well and where adjustments need to be made. Far too often, supervision is treated merely as a matter of supporting staff members and validating their frustrations. Supervision should of course include this, but it is ultimately unhelpful if the supervisor doesn't move on to target areas of performance that need improvement and then provide the help that will result in better performance. In some agencies, staff members and supervisors also monitor indicators of service quality, such as the number of scheduled meetings that clients have missed, and look for ways to improve on them—for example, by changing appointment times to better meet clients' logistical challenges.

- **Specifying the data that will, in each case and in aggregate, be used to assess the performance of the staff, of the program, and of the organization.** Organizations collect all kinds of data. Some are entirely due to funder interest and don't help the organization learn from its work and make adjustments to improve performance. Other data are essential to measure because without monitoring such information an organization will be limited in its efforts to learn from and improve its work. It is essential to clarify, for all levels of the organization, which data are serving which functions, and especially which data matter the most in assessing individual performance, program performance, and organization-wide performance—and, of course, how such data will be used in annual reviews and other mechanisms for holding people accountable.
- **Clarifying or designing the accountability system that will be used to manage the organization's performance.** The first step in designing and implementing an accountability system is to create competency-based job descriptions for all staff and management positions. I have yet to

encounter an organization that has such job descriptions in place when I first engage with them. Yet, without knowing that managers and staff have the requisite competencies to do their work well, it makes no sense to hold them accountable for working effectively. Just developing such job descriptions can take over a year to complete, and then they have to be implemented—that is, they have to be used when hiring new employees and in reviewing the performance of current employees. Implementation involves adopting ways to assess each competency, understanding what is required to help employees acquire new competencies or improve those in which they aren't proficient, and using individualized professional development plans designed for each employee's competency profile.

Once all this is in place, the foundation is laid to introduce accountability systems. Here the point is not to play "gotcha" with the staff, but rather to use accountability supportively to help staff members develop their competencies and improve their effectiveness. Among other things, it is very useful to establish which data will be shared transparently throughout the agency to highlight high performance and identify areas needing improvement. Further, the organization should make it clear how it will invest in targeted professional development to improve staff competencies and incentivize (symbolically and perhaps financially) high performance. As a final consideration, the organization must consider how long it will tolerate significant underperformance (in spite of sustained efforts to improve it) before staff members, managers, and leaders are reassigned or dismissed.

Here we have arrived in territory that, for many nonprofits, amounts to being a "stranger in a strange land." It is the facilitator's job to help workshop participants assimilate this way of thinking and, in the end, embrace it. In my experience, the best way to do so is to focus on the fact that, when all is said and done, we are collectively working on behalf of the organization's clients. They *need* the organization to develop in the ways I have been discussing because otherwise they won't be able to count on the organization to be a reliable partner in improving their lives and life prospects.

The final task of Day Four is to spend at least a half-hour helping the group process what it has experienced over the course of the workshop. Normally, participants are pretty exhausted by then. But I have found that often they are also exhilarated, because for the first time they have taken part in a sustained process through which they have been collectively creating a clear and achievable mission for the organization, meaningful goals and objectives, a well-defined picture of their target population, specific outcome "ladders" they will be helping clients to climb, codified programs and services with detailed operational expectations, and a newfound sense of cohesiveness and excitement: **"We're all in this together, and we're in it for our clients!"** They have become more aligned with one another, they understand what they and others are contributing to the organization's success, and they feel energized at the prospect of implementing, over the coming years, all the decisions they have reached.

More often than not, at the end I am told that although I may be abrasive (and perhaps excessively vulgar when attempting to drive home certain points), and the process has been at times painful and most assuredly exhausting, the experience is profoundly transformational—on both the personal and the organizational level.

Summary of Day Four

Once again, the facilitator asks the group to review the day's work and raise any issues that need to be discussed or clarified. Then the facilitator takes the group through the following steps:

1. **Specifying the criteria that the organization will use to select or improve its performance-management data system.**

2. **Clarifying the data sets that supervisors will review with front-line staff to help them improve the effectiveness of their work.**
3. **Specifying the data that will, in each case and in aggregate, be used to assess staff, program, and organizational performance.**
4. **Clarifying or designing the accountability system that will be used to manage the organization's performance.**
5. **Wrap-up.** This entails a review of the major decisions reached, and also of any decisions that will need to be made (and how they will be made). The facilitator then reminds the group of the need for the agency to develop a plan to implement the blueprint that the facilitator will produce. It is essential that the facilitator ask the executive director to lead this discussion so that the members of the organization experience the leader's commitment to the goal of moving the organization ahead.
6. **Stock-taking.** The facilitator should invite participants to reflect on the process and what it has meant to them. It is important to encourage the participants to acknowledge how challenging these discussions have been. The facilitator should join in this discussion, indicating where he or she feels it might have been possible to guide the discussion better, and thanking the participants for candid feedback as well as for trusting the facilitator to lead them through the process.
7. **Next steps.** The executive director should make clear what the next steps will be for developing an implementation plan, including who will be involved. It will be important to remind the group that such a plan will inevitably require three to five years to reach completion.

CHAPTER 5

From Introspection to Culture Change

At the end of the four-day workshop the organization will have made the kinds of fundamental decisions and clarifications that, if implemented, will allow it to perform reliably, effectively, sustainably, efficiently, and at a high level of quality. These decisions must then be captured succinctly and systematically in a document. The document should be the equivalent of an architect's blueprint: identifying key issues, specifying all operational metrics and needed actions, and guiding the next steps of the organization's development.

The blueprint is not an implementation plan. Once the blueprint is completed, the next phase of work is for the organization to map all the needed actions against timelines for completing them (i.e., to create a Gantt chart).[61] Then the organization will need to identify the resources that will be necessary to complete each item and consider how to develop and deploy those resources. In essence, such an implementation plan amounts to a business plan for building organizational competencies and capacity.

It is common for organizations to imagine that the implementation of their blueprint for performance management will be accomplished within a year or at most two. This is folly. In my experience no organization has successfully implemented such a blueprint in less than three years, and many require five years or more. When leaders and senior managers try to drive implementation too quickly,

61. The chart is named after its originator, Henry Laurence Gantt.

they put the organization under so much stress that the staff and lower-level managers will begin to undercut progress. The undercutting will not necessarily be maliciously motivated—it will be an expression of fatigue, and perhaps alienation that has been stimulated by unreasonable leadership expectations. (Some staff members might not even be aware of how their actions are affecting the organization.)

So, while it is fair to say that strong, sensible leadership and management is required during the organizational redesign work described in this book, perhaps even more wisdom is needed to lead the organization through the subsequent implementation of the blueprint—moving change forward quickly enough to secure the organization's future, but slowly enough to sustain its integrity through the transition process and beyond.

Implementing Performance Measurement and Monitoring

Organizations that are serious about implementing performance management must adopt a new motto: **"If it's not in our data system, it didn't happen."** Staff members and managers should not expect to be credited for undocumented activities, and the quality and quantity of their work should be assessed against clear performance standards using operational data. Here are some basic points:[62]

1. **It is essential to review each manager's and staff person's data entry weekly, at least in the first two to three months, until everyone enters data regularly without prodding.** Once that point is reached, leaders and managers should continue reviewing data entry on a regular basis (although the frequency might be reduced) as part of supervision and program management. After another three months, all managers and staff should be held accountable for the quality and completeness of their data.

62. With thanks to Ingvild Bjornvold of Social Solutions, Inc. for her help in compiling this list.

Example: Corporate leaders of Youth Villages review the performance data for front-line staff at every site no less frequently than monthly. Because they have branches in a dozen states, and keeping program quality at all sites high is so essential, they monitor for incomplete data entry, late data entry, and performance trends—at the staff, program, site, and regional levels. Managers are held strictly accountable for the quality of the data produced by their staff, and for maintaining upward performance trends or high performance levels.

2. **Key data sets, such as client demographics, staff activities, program participation, and client outcome information, must be reviewed for missing information or inaccurate entries.** Initially, staff who have not entered their data should be reminded to do so and shown how to correct mistakes. Leaders and managers should not make the corrections themselves, unless they plan to continue doing so forever.

   Example: Congreso de Latinos Unidos produces a report to identify gaps in clients' demographic information. The organization determined that the five demographics of race, ethnicity, gender, date of birth, and ZIP code are key fields that should be completed for all participants. Each month the agency's Data & Evaluation Department compiles the demographic "gap" report and provides it to divisional quality assurance managers to handle any necessary follow-up. Every two months, the Data & Evaluation team meets with the quality assurance managers to review the overall integrity of the data system, including this report as one component.

3. **Performance-management data systems must be useful to all staff—especially front-line workers.** The most compelling reason to implement a performance-management system is to improve the quality of work, effectiveness, and efficiency of the front-line staff—because this is the pathway to better results for clients. The process of ensuring staff buy-in to the system is never completed—and is critical. If the

staff find that the software is useful in organizing, tracking, and improving the results of their daily work, they are more likely to use it enthusiastically and well. This means designing easy ways for them to do data entry and retrieve key information, with "point of service" screens that help them monitor what they are doing with each client and see how well each client is responding, as well as to develop "to-do" lists and manage their work accordingly. Over time, frontline staff—and also supervisors and managers—will become sophisticated end users of the system and request additional functions to help them even more. Such requests should be given high priority!

Example: First Place for Youth in the Bay Area of California works with young people who age out of foster care. The agency provides transitional housing and intensive work on academics and work readiness. But the heart of its approach is case management, where these young people, often for the first time in their lives, are provided sustained relationships with caring and committed adults who, while holding the youths to high standards, give unconditional personal acceptance. First Place has found that these relationships move through stages of engagement. The youth workers (called Youth Advocates) use a scale that is built into the agency's data system to measure and monitor, weekly, the state of their relationship with each of the youths on their caseload. They and their supervisors refer to this information when reviewing cases in order to develop plans to help youths who seem to have become "stuck."

4. **Continue training staff after "going live."** Nobody retains everything they learned during initial training on a new data system, so refresher courses based on feedback and what the data reveal about training needs will be useful. Training is also an opportunity to build momentum and inspire the staff by showcasing not only positive client results but also staff members whose work is improving measurably.

Example: In 2011, the municipal job center in Esbjerg, Denmark, structured training for a staff of one hundred to introduce them to a new data system. The center used generic training sessions for groups of ten participants each, regardless of the program in which they worked. To this was added individualized training specially tailored to unique program needs. The training sessions are still ongoing, although they're held less frequently, several years after implementation—and front-line staff members are using the system effectively.

5. **Tie the staff's use of the performance-management data system to job descriptions and performance reviews.** While many staff members find that such systems offer great support in their work, others may need a little push. In the end, use of the data system by staff and managers at all levels of the organization must become nonnegotiable, and how well they do so should be assessed as part of annual performance reviews.

   Example: Roca, Inc., based in Boston and Springfield, MA, works with gang members and criminally involved youths. For years the organization had included "documentation of outcomes" in staff job descriptions, but there was no systematic way of keeping track of the degree to which they were doing this. Then the organization developed what it called the Staff Competency Framework. In connection with weekly supervision, program coordinators began to record in the data system itself whether the staff's data entries were complete and up to date, as well as each staff member's progress toward developmental competency goals (defined by the performance requirements of their respective roles in the organization). The chief of operations does the same for each division director and coordinator. The expectation was that building accountability into operations in a structured way would help people do their jobs better over time. And in fact it did.

My Hope

I wrote this book as a response to my perception that the social sector has failed, so far, to live up to its promise. While hundreds of thousands of social service organizations work incredibly hard to address our society's most intractable challenges and help structurally disadvantaged and socially marginalized individuals, families, and groups build better lives and life prospects for themselves and their children, few do so effectively. Indeed most lack the organizational competencies and capacity to do so.

As I've mentioned, to no small degree this failure is a by-product of an incredibly dysfunctional set of funding mechanisms where revenues come dribbling into the sector—literally as "billions of drops in millions of buckets" (Goldberg 2009)—without predictable standards and with no accountability on the part of funders to invest in agencies' organizational capacity to work effectively, reliably, efficiently, and sustainably.

However, there are courageous leaders of social service agencies who, in spite of these immense obstacles, are committed to delivering what they promise to the people they enroll in their programming. Such leaders need consultants and others who have the expertise to support them in their efforts to build up their organizations' performance-management capacity. I have had the privilege of working with a number of these leaders and their organizations, and also with some progressive funders who seek to change how they allocate resources, with a view to building up their grantees' organizational capacities and competencies. I have seen profound organizational redesigns and turnarounds—and the measurable benefits that clients have enjoyed.

But in my travels I have engaged with more than a few organizations for whom consultants had not been of much help—especially with regard to performance management. As I head toward retirement, I want to leave behind what I have learned for others to use—whether they are leaders, managers, or staff of direct-service organizations; funders; or consultants. My hope is that what I have written here—and share free of charge—will serve as a useful guide to any individual or organization working to improve the social sector . . . one organization at a time.

Which brings me back to the psychiatric hospital where my journey began. It was an enormous privilege to be entrusted with the challenge of leading an organization that palpably needed to improve. Patients had to wait far too long to be admitted, received an insufficient amount of active treatment, were too violent, stayed too long, and returned too quickly. Yet through a sustained collective effort that, in the end, depended on the buy-in of front-line staff, we managed to turn the hospital around. It wasn't easy. We all had to learn and grow. We had to put aside early tensions and build a new organizational culture with new expectations and performance standards, new ways of working. But the payoff was incredible. Patients were admitted immediately, received many more hours of active treatment, were much less violent, got better quicker, and stayed out longer. No one in the hospital earned a lot of money; no one received much by way of public recognition. But our collective exhilaration was real because, over a period of five to six years, we created a hospital where patients received what they needed and benefited more than anyone expected. Even two decades later, the work we did there remains one of my most cherished memories.

It is this experience, in fact, that has shaped my unshakable conviction that any organization with the right leadership and good advice can do the same.

Of course, every organizational leader or consultant has had a unique set of experiences that will shape how he or she approaches the task of implementing performance management. I have written this book to help them do this work creatively and productively, using their own experiences to continue to refine the methods and possibilities offered by this approach. I have seen that others can carry on this work, building on what I have shared and inevitably improving on it. I have seen some funders shift away from traditional grant-making toward what I call social investing, which includes investing in their grantees' performance-management capacities. Those who depend on the social sector desperately need these trends to continue.

APPENDIX I

Performance Monitoring and Evaluation: A Complementary Relationship

Performance monitoring often is confused with evaluation. While they are certainly related, there are real differences between the two. As discussed above in connection with Figure 1, both kinds of knowledge production are essential for high performance management.[63]

Simply put, performance monitoring is necessarily a forward-looking activity. It asks, "What are we accomplishing and how do we need to improve?" As an organization monitors and learns from its work, it will adjust what it measures and tracks in order to do a better job of managing its performance, strategically and tactically. Thus measurement is an iterative process, and its use and methods are viewed entirely within the context of the organization's work and its ability to drive performance toward the achievement of targeted results.

63. Developed in collaboration with Steffen Bohni Nielsen.

Table 6. Comparison of the Complementary Activities of Performance Monitoring and Evaluation

DATA-RELATED ACTIVITY	ITEM CHARACTERISTICS	PERFORMANCE MONITORING	EVALUATION BOTH FORMATIVE AND SUMMATIVE
Program planning, implementation, and management	Purpose	Evolving; iterative	Negotiated up front
	Focus	Broad; ongoing	Issue-specific; retrospective
	Timing	Constant/ongoing	Periodic
	Types of data collected	Inputs, outputs, outcomes	Inputs, outputs, outcomes, impacts
Obtaining data	Collector	Internal staff	External staff
	Collection intervals	Ongoing, "real time"—forward-looking	Rare—at large intervals (monthly/quarterly/yearly)—backward-looking
	Data validity	Presumed	Must be tested as part of the research
	Collection tools	Internal data (client demographic, staff efforts, client service utilization, outcomes), assessments, surveys, etc.	Desk research, public databases, interviews, observations, surveys, mining of information systems, new measurements using validated tools, etc.
Using data	Effectiveness	Causality of outcomes presumed for management purposes	Causality is a core issue that must be established scientifically; often a contribution analysis is more meaningful than an attribution analysis
	Organizational learning	"Real time" or ongoing	Infrequent—ex post facto
	Tactical utility	High ("real time" flow of data)	Low (very slow flow of data, often "stale")
	Strategic utility	Low to moderate	High
	Number of users	Many (all of the organization's leaders, managers, staff)	Few (mostly the organization's leaders and managers)

On the Validity of Performance Data

For the purposes of performance management, it is necessary to assume the validity of performance data. Hence it is essential for organizations to monitor the integrity (timeliness, accuracy, and completeness) of their performance data and eventually to test the validity through a formative evaluation (as discussed above).

In contrast, evaluation is backward-looking. It asks, "What has the organization done and accomplished? Does this meet our goals?" It provides the external reference points—including the use of validated measurement tools—to assess how well the organization's performance data capture reality (how valid they are). Measurements are designed up front, at the beginning of an evaluation, and then should be held constant for its duration (although admittedly there are many examples of evaluations that do not meet this standard—and hence are of questionable worth). Failure to hold them constant removes the high value of mapping performance data against a stable reference framework. (Imagine measuring your child's growth using an elastic tape measure where the length of inches and feet shift over time.)

Evaluation data are always *ex post facto* and "stale"—and thus their usefulness for tactical performance management is low. But they are extremely useful for holding an agency's performance data, especially regarding intermediate and long-term outcomes, up to the light of rigorous scrutiny—a function that gives such data great strategic utility.

With regard to tracking outcomes, it is important to highlight another way in which performance management and evaluation are complementary: **For performance-management purposes, it is essential to focus on short-term outcomes and the incremental progress that clients make toward them. In contrast, evaluations usually focus on intermediate and long-term outcomes because they are the measures of the value that an agency has produced.** Here short-term outcomes are seen as key inputs into the achievement of more enduring intermediate and ultimate outcomes.

It is worth briefly noting that there is a general sequence of evaluation activities that an organization should follow.

A Useful Sequence of Evaluation Activities

Step 1. Track performance data for several years until it is clear that the organization is enrolling the people it intends to help (target population) in its core programming, delivering the services in the ways and at the dosage levels it has specified, and achieving the outcomes it has targeted.

Step 2. Undertake an assessment of the reliability of the organization's performance-management system (data and the processes for using it to make adjustments in order to drive the achievement of results). Review the findings and make the organizational adjustments that are indicated. Take at least a year to test how well the organization has implemented these adjustments. Then, if they have been sustained and performance is high, it would be reasonable to move to the next step.

Step 3. Undertake an external "formative evaluation" that tests the validity of the agency's performance data regarding program enrollees, staff competencies, delivery of specified services according to implementation standards, and service recipients' achievement of short-term and intermediate (and, where the data allow, long-term) outcomes.

Step 4. Take the time to absorb the lessons of the formative evaluation and develop whatever plans are necessary to improve the areas of performance that were shown to be less than optimal (there are always some). This should identify specific organizational competencies and capacities, systems, and processes that will need adjusting to improve performance.

Step 5. Undertake a rigorous assessment to see how well the targeted organizational elements have been upgraded or advanced and whether the associated performance improvements have been achieved.

Step 6. Run the organization for at least another two years while sustaining high performance and program effectiveness as measured by service recipient outcomes. Repeat Step 5. If the organization has fallen short in any areas, make adjustments and then repeat Step 6.

> **Step 7.** Once the organization has been running at high levels of quality and effectiveness as specified in its implementation standards—in other words, it is meeting its performance standards as codified in its objectives—and has been able to do so for several years, the time may well be right for a "summative evaluation" that, among other things, tests the impact that the organization's services have had on the lives of participants. However, if the organization's scale of programming is too small for a rigorous evaluation to generate statistically significant data, the next step will be to grow the programming capacity to a level that supports a scientific evaluation approach—and then to repeat Steps 1 through 6 before moving on to a summative evaluation.

Unfortunately, few organizations and few funders are willing to exercise such discipline. Without it, evaluations will continue to be rigorous but useless—well measured but spuriously precise in their findings. The efficacy of programs and services to help participants gain targeted outcomes will be found wanting, but the fault may lie not in a weak model or approach but rather in the delivery of services by an organization lacking the capacity to manage performance strategically and tactically.

This, needless to say, is tragic. **It undercuts our ability to learn what works to help various populations improve their lives and prospects, and it gives us wrong ideas about what doesn't work.** Most tragic is that unless an evaluation[64] specifically looks at performance management, it will fail to identify organizational capacities and competencies that need to be developed in order to deliver programming reliably, efficiently, effectively, and at high levels of quality!

64. This is one way in which a formative evaluation can, depending on where an organization is in its development, be more useful than an impact evaluation. The former looks at key aspects of organizational functioning as well as the specific contributions of elements of programming to the production of outcomes; pure impact evaluations treat organizations simply as context, and tend not even to look inside programs to see how their elements work—hence the term "black box evaluation" that is often applied to such studies.

APPENDIX II

Pre-Workshop Worksheet

Several weeks before starting a theory-of-change workshop, the facilitator should ask the organization to complete a worksheet for each program—regardless of whether it is a core program intended to produce outcomes or a supportive program that only delivers outputs. This information will bring to the surface many of the issues that the workshop must address, and help the facilitator plan for the kinds of discussions that will be necessary.

Program Worksheet Introduction

At our upcoming Theory-of-Change Workshop, we will be discussing in depth both your organization as a whole and each program in particular. In order to understand the role that every program plays in furthering the goals of the organization, I will ask you to clarify for each of your programs whom you enroll, how you serve them, and what changes your program is designed to bring about in their lives. For each program please complete this sheet as best you can, and provide copies to everyone at the workshop. If you offer more than one program, please make sure to arrange for the completion of a separate worksheet for each (don't try to batch programs together). These worksheets will inform and help our discussion greatly.

Please note: It is important to fill out the worksheet to reflect, as accurately as possible, the current realities of your program delivery. For those programs not intended to produce outcomes, please don't try to develop a set of outcomes that you think might be good to claim. Examples of what might be called output programs include drop-in centers, resource centers, meals on wheels, homeless shelters, etc. Rather than imagining possible outcomes, simply say that this set of services is intended to provide a needed support or opportunity for clients but not to drive outcomes for them.

Worksheet

Program Name

Program Location(s)

Number of Program Slots

How many clients can participate in this program at any given time?

For instance, this could be the maximum number of individuals on a case manager's roster of clients on any given day.

Number of Participants Served Annually

How many clients does this program serve annually?

Unless a program is designed to last a minimum of one year and no one new is enrolled during that time, the number of participants a program serves annually should be larger than the number of slots it offers.

Target Population

Who gets enrolled into this program? Be as specific as possible.
Include demographics (like age, race, gender, and other things found on a census) and baseline characteristics (descriptions of your participants in the areas your program seeks to change). Examples of baseline characteristics: homeless, "at-risk" (specify for what), unemployed, drug-addicted, etc.

Program Elements

What services, supports, and opportunities does your program offer?
Examples: skills training, group therapy, case management, home visits, computer access, supported housing, transportation, medical screening and services, etc.

How does a client move through the program?
Example: How does someone gain access, get enrolled, be assessed, have a service plan developed, be monitored, and exit?

Frequency Elements Are Offered

For instance, if home visits are a program element, how often do they occur? Daily? Weekly? Monthly?

Or—how often is your front-line staff interacting with your program participants?

Outcomes

Not all programs produce outcomes. We will discuss the difference between Outcomes and Outputs during the workshop. If you think that this program is not designed to produce Outcomes, make a note of this and skip down to Outputs.

What changes in your clients' lives do you expect to result from their participation in this program?

These should be changes that are:

- *measured and monitored,*
- *sustained,*
- *linked to highly intentional staff efforts, and*
- *constitute what this program is held accountable for achieving*

Short-Term Outcomes

These are incremental changes that clients achieve in the course of their day-to-day program participation, and that can be thought of as "pathways" to the achievement of intermediate outcomes.

Examples:

- *New knowledge gained (e.g., knowledge of good parenting practices)*
- *New skills acquired (e.g., work-readiness skills)*
- *New behavior manifested (e.g., improved school attendance)*

Intermediate Outcomes

These are critical changes that clients achieve at key points in their program participation, culminating with criteria for deciding they are ready to be discharged from services—namely, the conditions you view as necessary and sufficient to create a significantly higher likelihood that clients will, at specified timelines after discharge, achieve targeted long-term outcomes.

Examples:

- *Consistent use of good parenting practices*
- *Grade promotion annually, culminating in high school graduation*
- *Transition from antisocial to pro-social peer group*

Long-Term Outcomes

These are the results of program participation that serve as the ultimate basis for assessing a program's value to society.

Examples:

- *Two years post-program discharge, completion of an associate's degree program*
- *One year post-discharge, success in keeping a job with promotion opportunities*
- *Two years post-discharge, not having been arrested for criminal behavior over the post-discharge interval*

Outputs

What products or activities does this program provide?
Some examples: pamphlets, meals, field trips, workshops, computer access, non-intensive mentoring/tutoring

Necessary Level (Intensity) of Participation

How many program elements do participants need? And/or, how often do they need to be engaged by these elements?

Duration of Program

How long is your program? What (if any) follow-up do you conduct afterward? What number and percentage of enrolled participants complete the program?

Please note any patterns you have identified with regard to who does and who does not complete the program.

Routine Referrals

Is there anything your participants need beyond what your program offers in order to achieve their outcomes?

For instance, if you are focused on teaching participants soft skills so that they can obtain and maintain employment, do you expect that they will also need hard-skills training, or childcare and transportation, for this to be a realistic outcome?

Front-Line Staff

Roles and Responsibilities

List the key roles for front-line staff in your organization? How many FTEs and PTEs fill these roles? What are the key responsibilities of each role?

Education and Experience

For each front-line role you identified above, what education, certification, and experience do you require?

Competencies

For each front-line role you identified, what are the core competencies?

Supervisory/Managerial Staff

Roles and Responsibilities

What are the key supervisory/managerial roles in your organization? How many FTEs and PTEs fill these roles? What are the key responsibilities of each role?

Education and Experience

For each supervisory/managerial role you identified above, what education, certification, and experience do you require?

Competencies

For each supervisory/managerial role you identified, what are the core competencies?

APPENDIX III

Web-Based Tools for Assessing Organizations

Many people who work in the social sector have suggested that it would be good to have some easy-to-apply tools that organizations and other interested parties could use to assess their strengths and capacities for managing performance—and also chart those areas that need further development. Similarly, there is also great interest in learning how to determine when an organization is ready to undertake either a formative or a summative evaluation. Recently I developed such tools. They are available on my website: www.dekh-consulting.com.

OMSAT: A Tool for Organizations to Assess Their Capacity for Managing to Outcomes[65] © 2012 Hunter Consulting

This tool yields valuable information to guide social service providers in their ongoing efforts to improve program quality and effectiveness. The tool is web-based, consisting of a thirty-question survey designed to enable leaders of social service organizations evaluate how likely it is that their own organization is "managing to outcomes"[66]—that is, whether its clients are apt to benefit as intended from the programming and services the agency offers. It looks at four domains of organizational performance that are essential to managing to outcomes successfully, each of which is defined by indicators as shown in the following table.

65. Produced by David Hunter to replace his Social Investment Risk Assessment Self-Assessment Tool (SIRASA) © 2011 Hunter Consulting, LLC—with the generous support of the Tauck Family Foundation.

66. A concept discussed in Mario Morino's inspiring book, *Leap of Reason: Managing to Outcomes in an Era of Scarcity* (2011).

ORGANIZATIONAL PERFORMANCE DOMAINS	PERFORMANCE INDICATORS
1. Strategic Leadership	**Clarity of Organizational Purpose (Mission)**—the organization's mission is specific regarding its purpose for existing, whom it serves, where it works, and what it expects to accomplish **Consistency in Holding to a Mission-Driven Course**—the organization has a history of keeping its focus on its mission, goals, and objectives and avoiding "mission creep"—especially in response to funder pressures
2. Outcomes-Focused Management	**Accountability for Outcomes**—the organization has clear performance standards and agreed-upon outcome measurements that it monitors and uses to understand and improve staff performance **Budgeting for Performance**—the organization deploys its resources with a focus on supporting areas that drive client outcomes (rather than, e.g., rigidly mimic categorical funding streams)
3. Performance-Management Capacities	**Data Integrity**—performance data are entered into the performance-management system accurately, completely, and on time **Outcomes Focus**—the organization tracks not only internal processes and outputs such as number of people served but also what results it achieves **Making Data-Informed Adjustments**—evidence that the organization has used performance data to make significant changes in its structure, capacities, staff competencies, systems and processes, programs, or other features in order to improve results **Relating Staff Activities to Client Outcomes**—evidence that the organization systematically reviews staff activities and the time spent in delivering them in relation to the results it is achieving
4. Program Effectiveness	**Delivering Programming with Fidelity**—the organization's core programming is codified and has both implementation and performance standards. Further, the organization monitors implementation and performance, making adjustments as indicated; hence it can be relied on to deliver its services at high levels of quality and in conformance with the design features of the program model—all of which suggests very strongly that the organization can deliver the outcomes that its programming is designed to create. **Evidence for Program Impact**—there is credible information to support the organization's belief that the kinds of programming or services provided actually produce client outcomes as intended

The tool's questions produce ratings in these five performance domains and the ten indicators that define them. It will immediately generate the following Reports once all thirty questions have been answered.

OMSAT Level 1

Contains an overall or global assessment of the organization's capacity to manage performance, an assessment of the four domains, and an in-depth look at the ten key indicators that define the Domains of Organizational Capacity to manage to outcomes—with a summary paragraph and a set of scores (scaled on a 100-point scale for each Indicator representing the level of organizational capacity to manage to outcomes).

OMSAT Level 2

Contains all the information of Level 1 plus an analysis of the responses to each of the thirty items, providing qualitative detail that deepens the understanding of the organization's capacities.

The numerical ratings make this tool very useful for leaders and managers of social service organizations to monitor incremental enhancements in their implementation of performance management, and improvement of the elements necessary for managing to outcomes.

Instructions for Using This Tool

To use this tool the executive director of the organization should assemble a team of key leaders, managers, and front-line staff to develop answers to the thirty questions. It is best if the questions are answered based on a group consensus. Where consensus is not achievable, the executive director (or a designated individual) should weigh the group discussion and decide how the particular item in question is to be answered.

All questions are multiple-choice and must be answered (the tool cannot be submitted with unanswered items; however, it can be "saved" as many times as necessary until all questions have been answered). Where the meaning of a question is not clear, the organization should make the best effort it can to interpret it and select a response.

A few questions should not be answered by the whole group, but only by those who have special knowledge that will let them to do so most accurately. These are specified in each case.

Some questions may require pulling together some information. If this requires interrupting the session, the tool will allow the organization to save what it has done and pause, then resume responding to its items.

Many of the questions focus on "core programming." This term refers to all programs and services the organization provides to members of its target population whom it has enrolled as clients and whom it expects to benefit by achieving specific outcomes. **Other programs or services should not be considered in answering these questions.**

Organizations with no core programming—that is, organizations with programs and services that are supportive or enriching in nature but are not meant to produce outcomes—should not use this tool. (Examples might include a drop-in center meant only to provide support or recreation, a creative/expressive program with no "teaching or skills-building agenda," or a soup kitchen that serves meals but does not link the people it serves to other services.)

OMET: Organizational Management Capacity Assessment Tool for External Analysts © 2012 Hunter Consulting LLC

Ideal for funders undertaking due diligence. Designed for an external evaluator, this tool consists of the same thirty questions as the OMSAT tool, but with judgments based on a detailed review of documents and performance data, as well as interviews of key leaders, managers, and staff. Instructions are provided regarding what to review and whom to interview before answering the questions.

The analyst receives the entire, detailed analysis—as well as numerical ratings—of key aspects of the organization's capacity to manage to outcomes.

A Quick, Nine-Item Assessment: Is My Nonprofit Organization Ready for Evaluation? © 2011 Hunter Consulting LLC

This tool is designed to help leaders (executive teams, boards of directors) of social service nonprofits—and interested stakeholders such as funders—assess an organization's evaluation readiness. **It is designed for organizations that wish to be accountable for client outcomes**, not just for activities and products (outputs).

When is an organization ready for evaluation?

It is ready when it can state clearly:

1. What groups or populations it is working to help
2. What results it is trying to help them achieve
3. What it is doing to help them achieve the targeted results
4. Whether the program participants or service recipients (clients) actually match the groups or populations it wants to be helping and how many are being served annually
5. What program or service utilization patterns are
6. Who fails to complete programming or use services as intended
7. What client outcomes are (both quantitatively and qualitatively)
8. That the answers to these questions have held steady for several years
9. That its performance data are complete, accurate, and entered in a timely manner

This tool consists of nine simple assessment items based on this list. **To answer these questions, an organization's leadership team should assemble and develop a consensus regarding the**

rating that best describes the organization as it is currently. The ratings and their scores will, when aggregated, result in a rating of a nonprofit's readiness for evaluation, and a suggestion for the kind of evaluation that would be most appropriate at this time—a **formative evaluation** that clarifies basic questions regarding the organization's implementation of programs or services and its capacities for delivering them reliably and in a sustainable manner, or a **summative evaluation** that clarifies the organization's social value and the impact of its work on targeted individuals, groups, families, or populations.

References

Buery, R. R., Jr. 2011. **"Keeping the Promise: A Blueprint for the Future of The Children's Aid Society."** Internal document based on Hunter 2011.

Coalition for Evidence-Based Policy. 2012. **"Rigorous Program Evaluations on a Budget: How Low-Cost Randomized Control Trials Are Possible in Many Areas of Social Policy."**

Coleman, R. L., and D. E. K. Hunter. 1995. **"Contemporary Quality Management in Mental Health."** *American Journal of Medical Quality,* 10 (3): 120–126.

Coleman, R. L., D. E. K. Hunter, H. Vartelas, and M. F. Higgins. 1996. **"Quality Management in Mental Health, II: Managing Risk of Dangerousness."** *American Journal of Medical Quality* 11 (4): 227–235.

Collins, J. 2001. ***Good to Great.*** New York: HarperCollins.

Collins, J. 2005. ***Good to Great in the Social Sectors.*** Boulder, CO: Jim Collins.

Feinstein, A. R. 1977. ***Clinical Biostatistics.*** St. Louis, MO: V. V. Mosby.

Gawande, A. 2004. **"The Bell Curve: What Happens When Patients Find Out How Good Their Doctors Really Are?"** *New Yorker*, Dec. 6.

Gawande, A. 2009. ***The Checklist Manifesto: How to Get Things Right.*** New York: Metropolitan Books.

Goldberg, S. H. 2009. ***Billions of Drops in Millions of Buckets: Why Philanthropy Doesn't Advance Social Progress.*** New York: John Wiley & Sons.

Grossman, J. B., and J. P. Tierney. 1998. **"Does Mentoring Work? An Impact Study of the Big Brothers Big Sisters Program."** *Evaluation Review*, 22 (3): 403–426.

Gueron, J. M. 2005. **"Throwing Good Money After Bad: A Common Error Misleads Foundations and Policymakers."** *Stanford Social Innovation Review*, Fall: 68–71.

Hunter, D. E. K. 2006a. **"Daniel and the Rhinoceros."** *Evaluation and Program Planning*, 29 (2): 180–185.

Hunter, D. E. K. 2006b. **"Using a Theory of Change Approach to Build Organizational Strength, Capacity and Sustainability with Not-for-Profit Organizations in the Human Services Sector."** *Evaluation and Program Planning*, 29 (2): 193–200.

Hunter, D. E. K, and S. Bohni Nielsen. Forthcoming, 2013. **"Performance Management and Evaluation: Exploring Complementarities—Editors' Note." In S. Bohni Nielsen and D. E. K. Hunter, eds.,** *Performances Management and Evaluation.* Washington, DC: New Directions in Evaluation.

Hunter, D. E. K., and M. Koopmans. 2006. **"Calculating Program Capacity Using the Concept of Active Service Slot."** *Evaluation and Program Planning,* 29 (2): 186–192.

Hunter, D. E. K. 2011. **"Children's Aid Society of New York City: Blueprint for Success with Key Elements of Programmatic and Organizational Redesign and a Framework for Performance Management."** Unpublished manuscript submitted to the Children's Aid Society.

Kusek, J. Z., and R. Rist. 2004. **Ten Steps to a Results-Based Monitoring and Evaluation System.** Washington, DC: World Bank.

Mayne, J. 2001. **"Addressing Attribution Through Contribution Analysis: Using Performance Measures Sensibly."** *Canadian Journal of Program Evaluation,* 16 (1): 1–24.

Miller, C. 2005. **"The Looking-Glass World of Nonprofit Money: Managing in For-Profits' Shadow Universe."** *Nonprofit Quarterly,* 12 (5).

Morino, M. 2011. ***Leap of Reason: Managing to Outcomes in an Era of Scarcity.*** Washington, DC: Venture Philanthropy Partners.

Penna, R. 2011. ***The Nonprofit Outcomes Toolbox: A Complete Guide to Program Effectiveness, Performance Measurement, and Results.*** Hoboken, NJ: Wiley.

Redcross, C., M. Millensky, and T. Rudd. 2012. **"More Than a Job: Final Results from the Evaluation of the Center for Employment Opportunities (CEO) Transitional Jobs Program."** OPRE [Office of Planning, Research and Evaluation] Report 2011-18. New York and Washington, DC: MDRC and OPRE, Administration for Children and Families, U.S. Department of Health and Human Services.

Snibbe, A. C. 2006. **"Drowning in Data."** *Stanford Social Innovation Review*, Fall: 39–45.

Tough, P. 2008. ***Whatever It Takes: Geoffrey Canada's Quest to Change Harlem and America.*** New York: Houghton Mifflin Harcourt.

Youth Villages. 2011. **"Youth Villages' Programs, July 2000 through September 2010."** Performance data published on the website www.youthvillages.org.

About the Author

David E. K. Hunter, PhD, started out earning tenure as an anthropologist, then left his university position to earn an MSW in order to work on the front lines in social services. Now he consults internationally to funders and social service organizations in the nonprofit and public sectors. He helps direct-service organizations develop results-driven strategies and theories of change (blueprints for success), build associated organizational capacities, and implement strategic and tactical performance-management systems. He also works with funders on implementing effective practices in social investing. And he speaks and writes about the challenges of creating, delivering, and assessing social value.

David's practice is grounded in over three decades of work in, and leading, social service organizations, as well as consulting. He has written and edited numerous books in the social sciences; his peer-reviewed articles and the papers he has presented internationally about nonprofit and public-sector performance management are highly regarded. The web-based tools he recently developed for nonprofit and public-sector agencies to assess their capacity to manage performance and take stock of their readiness for evaluation are available on his website: www.dekhconsulting.com.

David plans to retire at the beginning of 2014, which probably means that he will continue to take on a few strategically chosen assignments. But he will focus on spending time with his wife, Elaine, visiting their daughter, Lisa, and playing classical guitar. As Eliot Fisk once observed in a concert, "In the end all roads lead back to Bach!"

Afterword

If this book resonated with you and you'd like to engage in continuous learning on the topic of organizational performance, you can do so in all of the following ways:

- Visit my website (dekhconsulting.com) to get tools and tips for nonprofits, funders, and consultants.
- Get engaged with the *Leap of Reason* community.
  - Sign up for the *Leap of Reason* Update, a monthly newsletter that highlights new tools and resources for advancing leadership, innovation, and results-based funding: leapofreason.org/join-the-community.
  - Visit the *Leap of Reason* website (leapofreason.org) for copies of the book and access to a growing suite of materials.
  - Follow the *Leap of Reason* team on Twitter via @leapofreason.
  - Become a fan at the *Leap of Reason* Facebook page: facebook.com/LeapofReason.